*W*here is Heaven? Is it a physical or spiritual place? Do you have to die to get there? Why do some passages of the Bible refer to multiple Heavens?

These questions and many others are discussed in *God's Heaven Is a Real Place.* As you read each page, you'll feel like you're having a conversation with an old friend, someone who cares about you deeply and wants you to understand the truth.

There are clues scattered throughout the Bible about the reality of Heaven. Edward M. Smiling has gathered them all together, threading every chapter with scripture to illustrate the points he makes. It is his prayer that you will be blessed by the Lord through this book.

ISBN 9781537351179

9 781537 351179

God's Heaven Is A Real Place

Edward Marshall Smiling

coauthor/editor (Josellys Avila)
Final editor Neyra Smiling

ISBN: 1537351176
ISBN 13: 9781537351179

Contents

Dedication

This book is dedicated to everyone who lost a love one and wanted to know what really happen?

Introduction

Heaven is a real place, and ALL are welcome.

*B*efore I get started, I want to thank someone who is very dear to me, one who has inspired me like no one else—a person who is truly selfless. He was there with me from the beginning, before I could even read or write. When I thought this task would be too big, He kept encouraging me to write. He stayed on me, not letting me go until I started writing. When I wanted to quit, He said, "Keep going." He is truly a genius and really deserves all of the credit for this book. He is the most loving person you will ever meet. Although He is the richest man in the world, He loved me so much that He gave His life for me. With tears of love, honor, and respect flowing down my cheeks as I write this, I want to thank my dad and my best friend, Lord Jesus, the Messiah. Thanks, Dad—I love you!

What is Heaven? Where is Heaven? Who is in Heaven? Is Heaven real? If Heaven is real, how do I get there? These are all great questions that will be answered by the time you finish reading this book. You will have positive proof that there is a Heaven! You will understand the reality of Heaven! There will be no doubt in your mind that Heaven is a real place! Heaven is a real place with an address. It is a beautiful city where everything and everyone is perfect. By the way, a person does not always have to die to get there. Yes, that is not a misprint. Death is not the only way to get to Heaven. You can go to Heaven alive! But we will get into that later. Heaven is a real, physical place.

After you read this book, I trust that you will realize that the people in Heaven who chose to go to Heaven are alive! Yes, that's right—they are alive in Heaven right now. For example, your mother, father, sister, brother, son, daughter, aunt, uncle, wife, husband, grandmother, grandfather, friend, best friend, and anyone else who wanted to go to Heaven *is* in Heaven now, with GOD! Alive! Yes, that's right! Alive! They are not sleeping in their graves—they are alive right now, as we speak! The people in Heaven are able to see, hear, eat, drink, talk, and smell. They have a place to live, and they are PERFECT. For the Ladies who may be reading this book now, think about your body being perfect—perfect weight, perfect eyes, perfect height, perfect feet, perfect hands and legs, perfect hair, and not an inch of body fat. Not one wrinkle. Not one blemish! You will be yourself, but perfect. No need for dieting or exercise, and no bad hair days—ever! I am a bald-headed guy, and I am pumped up about that! Yes, I am excited about being able to have a perfect body in Heaven! In Heaven, we will be surrounded by the perfect LOVE of GOD. We will have a perfect mind, able to outperform even today's most advanced computers. "The greatest of these things is LOVE." In Heaven, love is perfect. The love for each other is perfect. The love of God is perfect! His love for you is perfect! There are no hidden agendas, no scheming—none of the phony love many of us have experienced in this day and age. For example, as some have stated, "Well, if you do this for me, then I will do that for you." This isn't love at all. In Heaven, love is simple but perfect. I will do it for you because I love you. God has made my love for you perfect, pure, and forever! I will always love Him, and I will always love you. Thus we will be able to have the most sincere and true LOVE for one another.

The Holy presence of God fills all of Heaven with love, joy, and peace. I guess you can say that in Heaven, my love for my BFF is PPF! Get it? Best Friend Forever with love that is Perfectly Pure Forever! In this book, I will make these truths about Heaven and GOD's LOVE for you so simple to understand that you will find yourself saying over and over, "That makes sense" or "Wow, I never thought of it that way."

By the way, be encouraged, and feel free to research everything you read in the following pages. You can look up the facts for yourself. They are backed up by the WORD Himself. Everything that you read in this book is backed by scientific evidence and the Bible, the Word of God. You can research all this stuff on the Internet or in your reference books and encyclopedias. My hope is that you will understand the reality of Heaven and God's unfailing love for you like never before. Later in this book, I will share some scientific truths backed by the Bible that will encourage and inspire your heart, mind, and soul. In the meantime, remember that Heaven is a real place that the Lord Jesus, the Christ, built for you. Do you desire reality and truth? Among the big hits during these past several years have been reality TV shows like *Keeping Up with the Kardashians*, *Naked and Afraid*, and *The Amazing Race*. Do you want reality? I will give you reality! I will share with you the best reality of all. Heaven is a real place! May the LORD bless your reading of this word! Let the journey begin!

CHAPTER 1

First and Second Heaven

*There is a man in Christ, who was once caught up to the Third
Heaven. Whether it was in the body or out of the body I do not
know, yet GOD knows. And I know that this man, whether in the
body or apart from the body, was caught up to Paradise. He heard
inexpressible things,
things that man is not permitted to tell.*

—2 Corinthians 12:2–4

Those are the words that the apostle Paul wrote to the Corinthian church in AD 55 to 57. The "Third Heaven"? What is Paul talking about? Caught up? Did he go to Heaven, came back, and live to talk about it? If he did, why does he seem unsure? He can't tell whether he was in the body or out of the body? Now, I know what you are thinking: "I am going to return this book and get my money back!" But please read on. I am building a foundation, laying the groundwork that will benefit you more later on than you realize. As I stated before, by the time you finish this book, it will all make sense.

Let's go back to when I wrote that death was not the only way to get to Heaven. Well, when Paul went to Heaven, (and later I will prove it), he was both shocked and confused after that amazing experience. Now, take a second to think about this. Paul's experience of Heaven was so awesome! So real that he was stunned, to say the least! Imagine—he actually saw the LORD JESUS! He also saw Joshua, Moses, and Elijah. He saw streets made of gold, the gates of the city made of pearls, and family members alive that he had buried and thought

1

were lost forever! There, in Heaven, *he saw them alive*! After all that experience, after seeing these things, it is no surprise that Paul was not sure if his experience had been in the body or outside of it.

Now, take a second, use your imagination, and think about this happening to you: You are placed in the finest spaceship, and you blast your way through many universes into Heaven. There at the landing pad you see the Lord Jesus. He calls you by name and says, "Welcome, my good and faithful servant. I love you. Enter into your rest." After you hear God's voice for the first time, He grabs you gently by the hand, and you can feel His deep love for you. After all these years you thought God hated you, but now you feel His presence, His love, and His peace so strong that you don't know whether to kneel or stand. Take another moment, and think about someone you loved who has passed away. When that person so dear to you died, your heart was filled with so much physical pain that you thought you would die. Perhaps you felt very angry at GOD. How could this have happened? Where had they gone? God, where were you? All these years, with so many questions in your heart concerning such matters. But now, as you enter Heaven, the LORD says, "Close your eyes. Turn around, now open your eyes," and that loved one is standing there, now alive, and you are so overjoyed because you had not seen them for years, and you thought you would never see them again. Now you are seeing them alive with their perfect body. Here on earth, we describe beautiful-looking people as drop-dead gorgeous or stunning. Well, that loved one is now so heavenly beautiful, totally perfect, and totally at peace with GOD and with everyone else who is also in Heaven. Those that were once buried with no legs are perfect with two legs. Those who were blind now see perfectly, never feeling that they missed out on seeing the things on earth because now they see complete, perfect beauty all around them. Those babies that were stillborn are now walking over to their parents and calling them Mom and Dad. The grandmas and grandpas that were buried because Alzheimer's finally took its toll, who died not remembering their own names, are now remembering their family, loved ones, and friends and have minds so brilliant they make our earthly professors look like toddlers in comparison. Now, *that* is some awesome news to hear!

I remember September 11, 2001, like it was yesterday. When those towers came down, it was such a tragedy, one we will never forget. I live in Queens, New York, and I can still remember the type of day it was. I can remember the smell of the burning towers throughout the city. I still remember seeing all those bodies being pulled out of ground hero. Yes, that's right—I changed the name from ground zero to ground hero (writer's liberty). A friend of mine, a firefighter named Benny, was in those towers, and he never came out. Imagine seeing loved ones who had lost their lives in the World Trade Center tragedy, now alive again! You thought they were dead, lost forever. You went through days, months, and most likely years of pain and tears. You perhaps were hurting so badly that you thought the pain from your broken heart was going to kill you. Yet, now you see them looking better than they've ever been before!

Now, after experiencing all this, you would probably be in a state of shock. Now can you understand why Paul seemed a bit overwhelmed? What Paul experienced was the reality of Heaven. It was Heaven in its full glory. Before Paul was converted, he had been a killer of many Christians. In Heaven, he saw those brothers and sisters alive! Needless to say, he had to be filled with great joy, yet surely he was stunned at what he was seeing.

Later in this book, I will go into great detail about what Heaven looks like and the type of bodies people have there. I will answer questions like "Are there angels there?" and "What's going on up there?" To understand Heaven, we need to find out what the MAKER of Heaven says. Then we can compare it to what we already know.

When GOD created the world, He used the plural word *heavens* to describe Heaven. And sometimes He used the singular word *Heaven* to describe the heavens. Genesis 1:1 states that in the beginning, God created the heavens and the earth. Notice the plural word *heavens* and not *Heaven* in this verse. That's because Heaven is one massive place with three different parts. I believe that God, in His great wisdom, decided to use the words *Heaven* and *heavens* to make it easy for us to understand that there is a real, live place called Heaven. GOD, in His Love for us, wanted to make it as simple as possible for you and I to believe in Him and His home, Heaven. Some of you only believe in things that you can see, feel, and touch. In fact, for most people, "seeing is believing." That is why Missouri is called the Show Me State. Because you got to show me! Keeping this thought process in mind, I am going to connect Heaven to what you can see so that it will be easier to believe the part of Heaven that we are so far away from and cannot see. By the way, here's a gentle reminder: not being able to physically see something does not mean it does not exist. For instance, most of us have not seen the air that we breathe, but we know that air does exist. To say there is no air just because you cannot see it would be foolish. If you took away all of the air that we cannot see, we wouldn't last five minutes! Some of us have never been to Europe or South America. To say that these places don't exist would be folly. Again, I live in Queens, New York, in North America. South America is connected to North America. To say that I do not believe there is a South America would be ridiculous. OK—now, getting back to explaining Heaven.

To keep it simple, I will do as the Bible does and explain Heaven's three parts. Let's call these three parts of Heaven; First Heaven, Second Heaven, and Third Heaven. Let's start with First Heaven. "The Heavens declare the glory of GOD. The skies proclaim the work of His hands. Day after day they pour forth speech; night after night they display knowledge. There is no speech or language where their voice is not heard. Their voice goes out into all the earth, their words to the end of the world. In the Heavens, He has pitched a tent for the sun." When we take a close look at this passage from Psalm 19, we see Heaven called "Heavens." As I stated before, God has made it as easy as possible for you and me to understand—understand that He is real, His unfailing love for you is real, and Heaven is real. Let me explain.

If you are reading this book inside of a building, take a walk outside. If you cannot go outside, then peek out of a window. Look up into the sky. You will see the clouds. The part of the sky that contains the clouds is called the First Heaven. We know that the first part of Heaven exists, because we can see it. If you have ever flown in an airplane, you actually flew through the First Heaven. God said in Psalm 19 that "the Heavens declare the glory of GOD. The skies proclaim the work of His hands."

The earth's atmosphere is made of 20.95 percent oxygen, 78.09 percent nitrogen, 0.93 percent argon, 0.03 percent carbon, and 0.03 percent other gases. This is perfect to sustain life on this planet. One with great knowledge,

God, has calculated and made this. Everything that you see, He did for us, because He loves you and I dearly. To say, "I don't believe that the first part of Heaven exists" would be foolish. We can actually see it. We live directly under it. And again, if you have ever flown in an airplane, you flew through it. The clouds and blue skies that you see are in the First Heaven. More importantly, God said it. "And God called the firmament Heaven. And the evening and the morning were the second day." Genesis 1:8

OK, just to recap: the first part of Heaven is called the First Heaven in the Bible. The first part of Heaven starts in our atmosphere where the clouds are and where planes fly. Hawaiian Airlines, JetBlue, and all airplanes fly through the first part of Heaven—the First Heaven. Now, let's move on to the second part of Heaven, called the Second Heaven.

When I was a child, the big thing in science class was the telescope. I can remember seeing them sold in every newspaper and magazine, similar to how they sell products today through cell phones, iPhones, tablets, and computers. The only tablets I knew about back then were the two that Moses brought down from Mount Sinai in the movie *The Ten Commandments*. Wow, how things have changed from when I was a child! Back then, reel-to-reel and eight-track tapes along with 45-r.p.m. singles and vinyl LPs were hot! And you had to have a landline. You young people, that is a phone with wires connected to your house. When I was a child, you had to carry your house around, or you could not talk on the phone, LOL! Back then, LOL didn't mean laugh out loud, either. Today, we have cell phones, Google Earth, and Curiosity on Mars! Oh, I'm sorry—I got a little off track. Back to the Second Heaven.

If you continue to look up while it is daytime and not cloudy, you will see the sun. If it is nighttime and not cloudy, you should see the stars and the moon. If you look through a telescope, you will see other planets. With satellites, you can see the Milky Way galaxy. As we advance in science and equipment, we find more galaxies and planets. The stuff we can see now with the knowledge we have is the second part of Heaven, called the Second Heaven. Our entire solar system is in the second part of Heaven. Our astronauts have gone in and out of the second part of Heaven all the time. The space shuttle was made to travel in and out of the Second Heaven. Our tiny planet is in the Second Heaven as well. Earth's atmosphere separates the First Heaven from the Second Heaven. To us, the second part of Heaven seems to get bigger and bigger. The more technology advances, the more we discover. The more we discover, the more we prove what GOD has already done. For instance, the word *firmament* really means "expanse." As we learn more, the Heavens seem to be expanding. We are finding more stars and more planets. On July 19, 2012, I read an article about scientists finding a new planet called UCF-1.01. The planet is thirty-three light years away. (By the way, I will share more on light years later.) The new world, as they call it, is in the constellation Leo the Lion. In fact, since 1995, scientists have found over seven hundred planets larger than Jupiter. (Feel free to research this if you'd like to.) The planets weren't lost, needing to be found. They were *already there*. To us, the universe seems to be expanding, but to God, it is already done! And—it's amazing that He did it in six days!

God saw all that He'd made, and it was very good. "And there was evening, and there was morning; the sixth day." By the seventh day, God had finished the work He had been doing, so on the seventh day, He rested. Think about a tiny ant being in your house, apartment, or condo. As it walks around your house, the place may seem to be huge and never ending. To you, the place is not big enough, yet to the ant, the place seems to get bigger and bigger. Take that same ant, and place it on five hundred acres of land with a fifty-room mansion. You get the point. To the ant, the mansion is extremely massive and never ending. It is the same with the Second Heaven. As we make better and more capable rockets, spaceships, satellites, technology, and so on, we are finding more in space. The more we find in space, the larger the universe seems to us. We do not have the capability to see it all. But just because we don't have the capability now does not mean it's not there. It is there, but we don't have the technology to get to it or to see it yet. Think about it: just thirty years ago, you didn't have a cell phone, laptop, or CD player, and soon even those may be obsolete. Until man landed on the moon over forty years ago, traveling in and out of space was not possible. Yet now we have space shuttles and space stations. When Christopher Columbus took sail, we thought that this earth was the only planet in existence. In fact, most people thought the world was flat, and they thought Christopher Columbus was crazy in believing the world was round. Some people thought that when Columbus set sail, he was going to fall off the end of the earth. At that time, if we'd told Columbus about the Second Heaven and that we would fly in and out of it at will, he perhaps would have thought we were not in our right minds. He would have called us the same thing that many people called him—crazy!

Now, we know that the Second Heaven exists because we can see part of it. If we look up, we can see the stars, the moon, and the sun. Also, our space team has flown over hundreds of missions in and out of the part called the Second Heaven. For people to say they don't believe in the Second Heaven just because they have not been there to feel or touch it would be foolish. It's like the ant on five hundred acres with a mansion. If the ant thinks its anthill is all there is—well, you guessed it: the ant would be foolish. The Heavens, as God called it, is so big, so colossal, and so huge that we don't have the technology yet to see it all. Most of the things we can see through telescopes and satellites are very far away from us. They are so far away that the distance is not measured in miles. The distance is measured by the time or years it would take you to get there if you were traveling at the speed of light. This is called light years. Now, light travels at 186,000 miles per second. In one minute, you have sixty seconds. In one hour, you have sixty minutes. In one day, you have twenty-four hours, and there are 365 days in a year. So, the speed of light travels about six trillion miles in one light year—5.88 trillion, to be exact. In other words, one light year equals six trillion miles away. Needless to say, one light year away in miles is *very* far indeed. The closest star to the planet Earth is Proximal Centauri. Proximal Centauri is four and a quarter light years—that's about twenty-five trillion miles away. The universe that we can see with our technology is thirteen billion light years across. This is as far we know with the knowledge that we have. Stop and think of that number—thirteen billion light years. In miles—well, you can do the math—it is very, very far. The galaxy that we live in is spinning at a speed of 490,000 miles per hour. But even at this superfast speed, it will take our galaxy two hundred million years to make one full rotation. There are over one billion galaxies in the universe. Now, above that, and so far away that we don't have a measurement for it, is the abode of GOD, the Third Heaven. This is the real place called HEAVEN.

OK—again, just to recap. The level of the clouds where planes fly is called the first part of Heaven, or simply the First Heaven. The place where you see the stars, the moon, the sun, or outer space is called the second part of Heaven, or the Second Heaven. Now, way above all things and so far away that we cannot see it with our puny earthly stuff is the abode of GOD—the Third Heaven, or simply Heaven.

CHAPTER 2

God Can Raise the Dead:
The Seed Gospel

*L*et us pray: FATHER, now this book will take readers into the part of Heaven where You are. LORD JESUS, bless these readers as they continue to read. Give them understanding and wisdom from Your HOLY SPIRIT so that they may comprehend the things they are about to read. Give them the courage to keep reading, and give to them spiritual eyes to be able to see the unseen. Touch their hearts, and let them be opened to You, LORD. Let them sense Your love for them like never before. Some of the readers need a miracle. We pray for their miracle, and we thank You, Father, because You hear our prayer. We know that when two or three are gathered in Your name, You are there with them, and You are here with us now. Touch the readers and their families like never before. LORD, while they are reading this book, You will be working on the things that concern them. Let them see the fruits of Your labor. Bless them, oh God. Where there is worry, give them peace instead. Where there is sadness, give them joy. Break every yoke of bondage! Heal them, oh God! Have mercy on them, and fill them with Your Holy Spirit! In Jesus the Christ's name I pray. Amen.

The third part of Heaven, or the Third Heaven, is where God is. For now, we will just say Heaven. This is the place that many of us dream about. This is the place where we all should want to go. Heaven is the place where we all CAN actually go to—if we want and receive that free eternal GIFT from GOD, the gift of ETERNAL life. In Heaven, there is no sickness! No fear! No death! No darkness! Just LIGHT! Only LOVE! Unconditional and never-ending love!

GOD's perfect love will surround us all, along with the beauty of His goodness and holiness!

Until now, we were dealing with Heaven in three parts. The LORD uses the plural word *Heavens* in the Bible so that Heaven would be simpler to understand. God is encouraging you to believe in the part of Heaven where He is, which you cannot see, by connecting it to the part of Heaven that you can see. If you have been reading this book from the beginning, you know that the first and second parts of Heaven do exist because we can see them. The Third Heaven, however, is so high and lifted up that we cannot see it. Since it is not visibly seen, some people find it difficult to believe in it—because they cannot see it. However, we all need to understand that just because we do not actually see certain things does *not* mean it is not there. For example, the very air (oxygen) that we breathe day and night for survival is not seen, but *air does exist*, regardless of the fact that we cannot visibly see it. So, just because we cannot see the Third Heaven doesn't mean it isn't there. HEAVEN is a real place, home of the LIVING GOD, CHRIST, our LORD. In Heaven, there are real, live people, living people—not just their spirits but their real, glorified bodies! One of the big myths is that Heaven is only a spirit place or that Heaven is only in the spirit realm. That may sound good, but that is not entirely true. Heaven is an actual, physical place.

It is understandable that some people find certain things difficult to believe. However, the eternity destination of many people is at stake—for those who choose not to believe. It would be foolish to think that GOD, who made our first home—the earth—couldn't make our second home with Him in Heaven. Of course HE CAN, and of course HE already has. Why is it hard to believe that the GOD who made the stars, moon, sun, the Milky Way, and our universe couldn't make a paradise for Himself and for us to dwell in with HIM? Think about it! Do you know what that sounds like? It's as foolish as if a man were to go on vacation and stay at the beautiful place called Trump Towers and then say to himself, "I wonder if Donald Trump, the builder of this beautiful hotel, has a place to live for himself?" Of course he has a place for himself! Yet that's what some people do with God. We live on and enjoy the earth that He created for us, we drink His water, and we breathe the air that He made for us, yet some may find it difficult to believe that He is and HE has a place of His own! Think about it! Some of us have been blessed to see some of the most beautiful places in the world that He created, like Hawaii, Cancun, and so on. People see our galaxy, our universe, and then they say they don't believe God could make Heaven. They don't believe there *is* a Heaven, and worse yet, some don't want to believe that there is a God. Come on, now! GOD says, "The fool hath said in his heart, there is no God...The LORD looked down from Heaven upon the children of men to see if there were any that did understand, and seek God." (Ps.14:1–2). (By the way, for you gamers out there, that "Ps." stands for the book of Psalms in the Bible, not "play station"!) In essence, God has made it so easy for you to believe that He says you are being a fool if you don't.

Again, Heaven is very far from the earth. There is nothing manmade that will take you there. There is nothing manmade that is able to measure the distance from Heaven to earth. To prove a point, let's say that Heaven is 777 trillion light years away. Now, please remember that only GOD and those who are in Heaven know the real distance from earth to Heaven. But to make a point, if Heaven were only 777 trillion light years away, we would burn up trying to fly a rocket ship there. The ship would have to travel as fast as or faster than the speed of light. Think about it—have you ever seen lightning in the sky? Lightning travels at the speed of light, and as you already know, light travels really fast. Remember light years? As I explained earlier, one light year equals the distance of about six trillion miles long (5.88 trillion, to be exact). To get to Heaven, we would need to travel much faster than lightning! I believe that Heaven is much farther away than my puny guess of 777 trillion light years.

So, the question is: How do I get to Heaven? There are two ways to get to Heaven, but there is only one way to get *into* Heaven. I will repeat that again. Please read this part slowly: there are two ways to get to Heaven, but only *one way* to get into Heaven. For instance, there may be many ways for me to get to your house. I could take the highway, or I could drive through the local streets. Since I ride a Harley-Davidson V-Rod, I could come by motorcycle, or I could take a cab to your house or take the bus. I also perhaps could take the train to your place, but once I get to your house, you have to let me in. I could ride my motorcycle to your front door, and yes, although I stand at your door and knock, if you don't open the door, I cannot come in. Likewise, there are two ways to get to heaven. You can die and go to Heaven, or God can translate you to Heaven alive. Once you get to Heaven, though, there is only one way to get inside the city.—GOD HIMSELF has to let you in. In line with my theme of keeping it simple, let's break this up into two parts. First we will deal with dying and going to Heaven. Then we will deal with going to Heaven alive. Hence, the name of this chapter: "God Can Raise the Dead: The Seed Gospel."

OK, let's deal with the easy part: death. I am going to make three of the boldest statements you probably have ever heard. Statement number one—God can raise the dead! Statement number two—you can live forever! And last but not least—I can prove it! Let's make these three into one: God can raise the dead, you can live forever, and I can prove it! God so loved the world that He gave His only begotten Son, that whosoever believeth in Him shall not perish but have everlasting life! Now, here is the challenge to you. If I can prove to you that there is life after death and that God can raise the dead, I want you to put your faith in God and give your life to Him. Here is the best part: if I prove there is life after death and you give your life to God, He will give you everlasting life! It is the deal of eternity! Trust God, and you get to live with Him and your family in Heaven forever!

Now, think about the money that a lot of movie stars spend on trying to live forever. Some of you reading this book are very rich and famous, spending millions of dollars on plastic surgery and Botox, trying to look perfect. Yet you are never satisfied with the way you look. And even if you're close to perfection, a longing remains in your heart that leads you to think there must be more to this life! Deep down, you know that on this planet, you may have up to 120 years of life—at most. Then what? Not only is GOD offering you eternal or everlasting life, but HE can also grant you life more abundant here on earth as well. Now, that is a deal you should *not* refuse. Where you will spend eternity depends on your decision now—while you are still here on earth, living this temporary life. Your choice needs to be made while you are still alive now. God offers forgiveness of sins, a clear conscience, and most importantly—life forever with HIM, and you will also be able to enjoy life forevermore with everyone who believes as well. If I can prove it to you, everlasting life would have cost you only the price of this book! You will live FOREVER! Living forever with GOD, who loves you! And why wouldn't God love you? It seems simple to understand that if someone wants you to live with him or her forever, then he or she must really love you. By the way, I think you should put your faith in God just because He is God—period! But for my people from Missouri, if I prove there is life after death and that God can raise the dead, then you will give your life to Him. If I don't prove there is life after death and that God can raise the dead, then you don't have to do anything but keep reading this book, because I am sure you will change your mind later. Remember, we are just knocking on Heaven's door. We still have to go inside. When I describe what is inside the city in which you will live, you will want to go there. Besides, don't we all want to live with the living, loving, kind, wonderful, majestic God forever?

GOD can raise the dead? YES, GOD can raise the dead, and I can prove it! What a profound statement! In fact, every one of us has seen God raise the dead. He has done it so often, and it is so common that we take it for granted (we will discuss more on this soon). The apostle Paul was also faced with the same question in AD 55. Some of the people of that day did not want to believe what Paul said when he stated that JESUS the CHRIST was alive. Many of us know that Jesus was brutally beaten and crucified for your sin, my sin, and the sins of the world. After three days, Jesus rose from the grave. That's why each year, we celebrate Good Friday—to remember the day that Jesus died for us on account of His great love. Then at Easter (Resurrection Sunday), we rejoice greatly, remembering the day Jesus rose from the dead. After rising, Jesus appeared to a man named Cephas. After that, He went to visit with the twelve disciples and others for forty days. On His way to see the disciples, He appeared to the two Marys: Mary Magdalene and Mary, the mother of James. In fact, what a lot of people don't know is that Jesus was seen by over five hundred people at once after He had come back to life. Here is Paul's answer to those who said there was no resurrection from the dead:

> Do not be misled: bad company corrupts good character. Come back to your senses as you ought, and stop sinning. But

someone may ask, "How are the dead raised? With what body will they come?" How foolish! What you sow does not come to life unless it dies. When you sow, you do not plant the body that will be, but just a seed, perhaps of wheat or of something else. But God gives it the body as He has determined, and to each kind of seed He gives its own body. All flesh is not the same: human beings have one kind of flesh, animals have another, birds another, and fish another. There are also heavenly bodies, but the splendor of the heavenly bodies is one kind, and the splendor of the earthly bodies is another. So will it be with the resurrection of the dead. The human body that is sown is perishable, yet it will be raised imperishable. It may be sown in dishonor yet raised in glory. It is sown in weakness, yet it will be raised in Power. (1 Cor. 15:33–43)

OK, here is what Paul was saying: The proof that God can raise the dead has been right in front of us, and we've never thought about. It is in the seed. What you plant in the ground does not grow into a plant unless it dies first. A person may place a dead seed into the ground, yet it is God who brings it back to life and gives it a new body like the plant it was before it died. If a person plants a dead grass seed in the ground, out comes a beautiful lawn. One may plant dead tomato seeds in the ground, and then God will raise from that seed a live tomato plant and tomatoes.

Here is another and perhaps the most important example: A man may bury his mom's or dad's body, yet God sends angels to collect their spirits and bring them to Heaven. In Heaven, God gives them brand new bodies that are perfect. We bury flesh that will turn to dust, and then in Heaven, God provides a glorious body that will never die. Just like He gave the seed, God gives our loved ones new bodies. The old bodies are laid to rest in the ground. In Heaven, our loved ones have new bodies that are perfect in every way and that will never die. The grass seed or tomato seed doesn't look anything like the new plant. The seed is dry, it's withered, and it's dead. But when the new plants come, you know that some are grass and some are tomatoes. You can see the difference.

The same happens with us: we bury bodies that are imperfect and have no life, yet the new bodies that GOD gives people are perfect and will live forever, and we will know each other and see the difference!

Before I go any further, think on this: If God can give you the body that you have now, what makes you think He can't give you another one that is perfect? He gave you a body already through two imperfect humans (your mom and dad), and you are living proof of that. So He is definitely able to give you a new, perfect body all by Himself.

Do you want more proof? If you have a sealed package of grass seed (or tomato seed, pumpkin seed, etc.), you can use that as a visual aid to help you understand. If you don't have any type of seeds, please get a plastic Ziploc bag, or any bag will do. Put something in the bag and then seal it closed, pretending it is seed. If you don't have anything, I have a sealed bag of Wonderlawn Kentucky bluegrass seed that has never been opened, so please follow along in your mind. Now, imagine my sealed bag of grass. It is a two-pound bag that has never been opened. It is sealed tight so that no air, water, or soil can get into it. It has been that way since the day I bought it. For those of you who have an actual seed package, I want you to take that package into your hand. When you buy grass seed, it is usually in a sealed box or plastic bag. Now, look at the sealed bag. The bag is sealed off from the air. Now, ask yourself this: "Can anything live without air?" The answer is no.

Look at the bag again. The seed in the bag is sealed off from soil, which contains food for the seed. Now, ask yourself this: "Can anything live without food?" The answer again is no. Last but not least, every living thing needs water. In fact, all living creatures are made up of a percentage of water. Water is essential for life. Look at the package one last time. Notice the package is sealed off from water? Ask yourself this: "Can anything live without water?" The resounding answer is no. The seeds in the package are—you guessed it—dead. Now if you and I were to take our grass seeds, tomato seeds, and pumpkin seeds out of their packages so that they could have air to breathe and then put them in the ground so that they would have food to eat and then pour water on them so that they would have water to drink, then God by His Holy Spirit will raise the seed from the dead. You plant a dead seed, but GOD brings it to life. We may bury the lifeless bodies of our loved ones for whom we cared so much, like a mom (like I did), or a dad, son, daughter, brother, sister, friend, aunt, uncle, grandma, cousin—whomever—then GOD by HIS HOLY SPIRIT raises them from the dead and gives them a new body that will never die. That's why CHRIST JESUS, when talking about His pending death on the cross, said, "The hour has come for the Son of Man to be glorified. I tell you the truth, unless a kernel of wheat falls to the ground and dies, it remains only a single seed. But if it dies, it produces many seeds." (John 12:23-24) the LORD used the seeds as an example that you can hold in your hand and see that He has the power to raise you and anyone else that believes in Him. HE has ALL POWER and AUTHORITY to RAISE our bodies from the dead. JESUS knew that His single death would save many lives for GOD. Again, the theme throughout this book is that God has made heavenly things so simple to understand, by what we already know, that even a caveman would believe it! Look around you. GOD created this world out of nothing, so raising the dead is a piece of cake for Him. When people die, they take their last breaths on earth and their next breaths in Heaven. Once in Heaven, you will receive a new body, and this happens in an instant—yes, quicker than the snap of a finger.

Before I get more into the everlasting, I encourage you to do something that is of the highest importance. Now that you have read this far about what I believe to be excellent proof that GOD can raise the dead, I strongly and fervently suggest that you give your life to the LORD, if you have not done so already. When you give your life to Him, He will give you His Holy Spirit. The HOLY SPIRIT is His guarantee that you will live forever! HE will remind you that you belong to GOD and help you realize that you are a part of Him. Think of it this way: HE in you, and you in HIM. You'll be at peace and one with GOD. Not only does God want you to live with Him forever, He also gives you HIS SPIRIT as a guarantee! (For He cannot deny Himself.) By the way, the Holy Spirit Himself will help you understand the rest of this book.

Now, most people do believe that when they die, they will go to Heaven. Many do hope that there is something after death. Deep in their hearts, they all know that this life could not be all there is, and that is rightfully so. Yet some may find it more difficult when they start reading about going to Heaven alive.

If that is the case with you, then you need the Holy Spirit to help you understand this. Have you thought that the first part of this book was hard to comprehend? Well, the truth is that without the Holy Spirit, the rest of this book may be too much for you to handle.

GOD is HOLY. The Bible states that without holiness, no one can see God. Notice the key word *Holy*. Here is humanity's problem: God is Holy, yet in and of ourselves, we are not. God is pure; we are not. God is righteous, and we are not. Heaven is a place that is Holy, but we are not. Heaven is a place that is pure, the home of the righteous, yet we are not. God loves us very much, but He hates sin. We love to sin, and some of us do not like God. Some of you even hate God. God despises sin because it separates us from HIM, and it can kill us. We like to sin because we think it is fun. Here is an example. We like the sin of harming our bodies by smoking cigarettes, and we think it is fun. God loves you, but He hates that sin because it can give you lung cancer and kill you. We think that God is just this mean old guy not hip with the times and trying to take away our fun. But God loves you so much that He made manufacturers put cancer warning labels on cigarette packages because He doesn't want to see you hurt. If the cigarette doesn't kill you, you may end up having to live with one lung, no tongue, a hole in your throat, no teeth, missing toes, fingers, and so on. This isn't how God wants you to spend the rest of your life. God love you very much and only wants good things for you.

GOD loves everyone, yet He hates any act of self-destruction. He created people to have life and have it more abundantly.

Humanity as a whole sometimes has had the false thought that GOD is trying to take away anything that is fun. But again, like with the cigarettes—manufactures now put warning labels on the packages because of the harm they will cause—the LORD does not want to see anyone hurt, so He made sure the laws of the land were placed so that boundaries in general wouldn't be crossed. If anyone chooses to ignore any warning, then surely consequences will follow. By then, no one should ever try to blame God for the consequences that people themselves chose, even though many eventually do.

Here is another example. Hammer time! In New York, we like the sin of going to the bar and getting hammered! For the benefit of everyone in the country reading this book, it is called getting drunk. In New York, it's hammer time. God loves you, but He hates the sin of drunkenness. Again, we think God is a killjoy who doesn't want you to have any fun. But God knows that if you get drunk and then drive, you can kill yourself and others. Many of us have enjoyed the sin of getting drunk. Some of us have liked going out to the bar to "get hammered"—yes, getting drunk. GOD loves you and me, but He hates the sin of drunkenness. Another of the effects of the sin of drunkenness is that alcohol can destroy a person's organs, filling their last years on earth with extreme pain. The funny thing is that deep down inside, people know that GOD is right. That's why when we get in trouble or too drunk, we cry out to God, "Oh Lord, please! If you help me this one last time, I will never do it again!" Toilet bowls all over the world have heard similar prayers. They have been heard in every language.

GOD is righteous. Consequences follow the unrepentant sinners. If He didn't punish sinners, then Hitler would have gotten away with six million murders. No matter how much fun it is to sin, consequences will always come. For example, if a man is fooling around with someone else's wife, the husband's anger just might lead him to kill her and the other man. If the husband doesn't get him, then most likely some type of sickness—AIDS and/or some other disease—just might. Because God is righteous, He can't let anyone keep sinning without being punished. When you really think about it, sin is easy but ends up being hard work. We all want to be paid for our hard work. We all should get our wages for sin—we deserve it. I mean, you don't want to do all of that work for free! Everyone wants to be paid their wages, right? Well, the wages of sin are death, hell, and separation from God. Well, I don't want that payment, and you don't want to be paid like that. So, we need a savior! Someone that will die to take my place so I don't have to.

We know that at some point in their lives, our loved ones who are now in Heaven understood this big problem and made their peace with God. With their last breaths, some cried, "Jesus, forgive me!" And, by the way, if people think to themselves that they will wait until their last day on earth to repent, well...the truth is that tomorrow is not promised to anyone. CHRIST JESUS came and took our place, and when He died on the cross, He paid for my sin and your sin once and for all. In fact, He paid for the sins of the entire world—yes, everybody in it. He died so that you don't have to die. He was pierced for our transgressions, He was crushed for our iniquities; the punishment that brought us peace was upon Him, and by His wounds we are healed. He died so that we can go to God and receive His forgiveness. Jesus is your payment for sin. Jesus is your way into Heaven, and He makes us at peace with GOD Himself. That is why Jesus said, "I am the way, the truth, and the life. No one comes to the Father except through me." (John 14:6) "I tell you the truth, whoever hears My word and believes Him who sent Me has eternal life and will not be condemned; he has crossed over from death to life." (John 5:24)

Look at how badly God Loves and wants you! We sin, and God should destroy us, yet He came up with a way to pay for our sin without punishing us. Think of it this way: I have two twin daughters, for example, and if one makes a mess, and the other wants to clean it up, I have no problem with that. The place still gets clean. The one twin took the place of the other and cleaned up the mess, and I—the dad—am happy. So, picture this: CHRIST JESUS is your twin for sin. Although He was sinless, He took your place along with the punishment that you and I deserved! With sin, we have made a mess of our lives. Jesus paid for our sin and cleaned up our mess, and He will continue to clean us up. All God wants is for us to believe in what HE has already done for us, turn from our sin, ask for His forgiveness, and thank Him for what He has done. Then God won't have a problem with us.

Think of it this way: SIN stands for "Stop It Now"! For my young readers, here's another made-up example. God wrote the SAT and gave you the answer to the test, so to speak! The ANSWER is CHRIST JESUS! Be SAT, which stands for "Saved for All Time."

OK, here's another opportunity for those who have not yet received the LORD's forgiveness. Take this time to pray and receive by faith the forgiveness for your sins and RECEIVE HIS HOLY SPIRIT. Pray this out loud if you can. If you can't, then just pray in your mind as you read:

> LORD, I need your Help. I am a sinner who needs forgive-
> ness. I choose to believe by faith that CHRIST JESUS died for

my sin and that HE rose from the dead and is alive in Heaven. I put my trust in YOU, LORD, and I ask that you forgive me for my sin. HOLY SPIRIT, I ask that You come, live in me, and empower me. Strengthen me to live this life for You in your righteousness, and help me live for Your glory, that I may help other people in their time of need as well. In CHRIST's name I pray. Amen.

If you prayed that prayer above, this is the best day of your life. You might have felt HIS loving presence while praying, or you may have felt nothing at all. Yet no matter what, the bottom line is that you are GOD's child forever, and He will start to do amazing things in your new, changed Life. Feel free to mark this date and time on a calendar or in this book—you may want to remember it. Again, this is the best day of your life, and you will never be the same!

If you did not give your life to the LORD yet, keep reading; you may get another chance. But I would ask you to think about this: You may work for a large company or a small business, and on your job, whatever the head of the company says goes. If you try to do whatever you want and not follow orders, you will be fired. You don't tell the boss on your job, "Well, I don't believe that it has to be this way." At work, you do what you're told, or you'll soon be out of a job! For those of you who are CEOs of companies, what if your employees came to you and said they don't like the way you do things? Most likely you would fire them in a minute. To think that someone who works for you would have the nerve to tell you that they will not do things your way! Some of you CEOs are getting angry right now just at the thought of it! Here is my question for all of us reading this book: How do you or I or anyone get to tell GOD that what HE has already done for us all is not enough? What JESUS CHRIST paid on the CROSS is MORE than ENOUGH. Think about it: HE is the CREATOR of the entire universe, far greater than mankind, much greater than your boss or the kings of this world—He is the Creator of mankind. Think about what Jesus went through for you. If you saw the movie *The Passion of the Christ*, then you got a small taste of what Jesus went through for you, because if you read your Bible, you would understand that for the sake of Hollywood, Mel Gibson actually held back. In fact, before he released the movie, he showed it to some of the top religious leaders and teachers. Some of them told Mel that they thought he went too far. Mel told them he'd been holding back, and he asked them if they'd read their Bible, because JESUS went through a lot worse than the movie could show!

I realize that some people reading this book right now may believe, yet there are also others who may say to GOD, "No thanks. You sacrificed CHRIST, your Son, for nothing. I worship God in my own way. I will pay for my own sin." (By the way, you can't, pay for your own sin and you don't want to, not even at minimum wage) Please think about this carefully. I suggest that you go back and pray the prayer and then continue reading with the rest of us. Go ahead—we will wait for you. Receiving God's love and forgiveness is worth it!

If you did pray, and you did give your life to the LORD, I am so happy for you! Yes, I rejoice for you greatly. I want to be the first to welcome you into the kingdom of God as a man, woman, or child of God! Awesome! When you said that prayer, not only did all of Heaven rejoice—GOD rejoiced all the more! You now have the Holy Spirit of the living GOD living in you! You now have eternal life! Awesome! GOD has already marked this day down. Yes, the LORD has written your name in the LAMB's book of life, and all of Heaven can read it. You should write this day down also, because from this day forward, your life will never be the same! CHRIST is the LAMB of GOD that takes away the sins of the world.

CHAPTER 3

What Happens When I Die?

Congratulations!! You now have everlasting life. You now have eternal life—yes, now you will live forever. Up until now, we have been dealing with things that we can look up and see. Some we can see with our natural eyes. Some we need instruments to see. Yet now, we are going to deal with things that are so far away we cannot see them—the unseen. If you have a Bible, now is the time to get it and have it nearby. The Bible is our best resource on Heaven and everlasting life. I will be using a lot more scripture, and you may want to cross-reference.

As we now know, when you give your life to the LORD JESUS CHRIST, after you die in the natural, you will go to Heaven. Many people believe that the only way to get to Heaven is to die and go to Heaven. So, exactly what happens when a person dies? The better question is, does a person really die? The answer is NO. You will never die. Remember—GOD says that whoever believes in HIM has everlasting LIFE.

This book may get more challenging to understand, but we trust that the Spirit of GOD will help you understand. Again, it is wise for you to take some time now to receive Christ Jesus as your Savior by asking Him in prayer, if you have not done so already. With all your heart, ask Him to forgive you of all your sins and cleanse you spiritually. Receive His love by faith, and ask His Holy Spirit to help you understand the rest of this book. We all need the LORD in our Lives, and it is extremely important for each of us to receive ETERNAL LIFE through JESUS CHRIST. If you already stopped to pray, again I remind you that you just made the most important decision of your life! My heart is filled with joy for you!

I will tell you this TRUTH: you are the reason that the LORD led me to write this book. All of Heaven is giving you a standing ovation. They are celebrating your wise decision. CHRIST JESUS said, "I say unto you that likewise Joy shall be in Heaven over one sinner that repented" (Luke 15:7). We PRAISE our LORD for that. When it's time for the believer to go to GOD in Heaven, there the LORD gives the believer his or her new glorified body—a perfect body.

We are going to look at some different passages of scripture. I will quote some of the verse and then explain what you just read.

Let us start with 2 Corinthians 5:1–8. It begins, "Now we know that if the earthly tent we live in is destroyed, we have a building from God, an eternal house in Heaven, not built by human hands."

OK, here is what this verse is saying. It simply states that if our earthly body dies, we have a new body from God that will live forever. The building that he is talking about is your body—a body that is eternal in Heaven, not built by human hands.

Let us continue to verses 2–4: "Meanwhile we groan, longing to be clothed, with our heavenly dwelling, because when we are clothed, we will not be found naked. For while we are in this tent, we groan and are burdened, because we do not wish to be unclothed but clothed with our heavenly dwelling, so that what is mortal may be swallowed up by Life." What verses 2–4 are saying is that we desire and long to put on our new bodies from Heaven, because when we are clothed with our new bodies, we will not be found naked as spirits without bodies. For while we are in these earthly bodies, many times during our lives' tough circumstances, we groan and are burdened, wanting to get out of these bodies and into our new bodies from Heaven.

By the way, I am recently recovered from prostate surgery. I had cancer. By the grace of God, I was blessed with one of the top surgeons in the country, and he took out my prostate and got all the cancer. Dr. Vincent P. Laudone, if you're reading this book, God bless you! And you too, Nurse Anne! Yet, as great a job as they did, I still groaned, wanting my new body, because recovery was very painful. There were times I thought about being in Heaven with my new body from GOD. But here I am, still here, writing this book, yet I had no fear of death. In fact, I was dying to be with GOD—no pun intended! Yes, and I still look forward to the great day when I will be with my SAVIOR! But for now, I do thank GOD that I am still here on this earth, because my family and friends need me—and I need to finish this book for you. With lots of love and prayer, I write this book so that you may have knowledge of GOD's Love and TRUTH that will set you FREE from the fear of death.

Now, continuing with the scriptures and finishing up verse 4: "Because we do not wish to be spirits with no bodies or unclothed, but to be clothed with our new body from Heaven, so that when what is mortal dies, I will get a new body; with my new body I will live forever!"

The key here is that when you die, God gives you a brand new body from Heaven. The people in Heaven have real bodies that will last forever! They are bodies that you can see, feel, and touch—they are not just spirits! They are able to eat and drink as you and I do.

Let us move on to verses 5–8. "Now it is God who has made us for this very purpose and has given us the Spirit as a deposit, guaranteeing what is to come." (Remember I told you earlier that the Holy Spirit, the Spirit of Jesus, is your guarantee that you are going to Heaven?) "Therefore, we are always confident and know that as long as we are at home in this body, we are away from the Lord. We live by faith and not by sight. We are confident, I say, and would prefer to be away from the body and at home with the LORD!"

Verses 5–8 explain that GOD has given us His HOLY SPIRIT as a deposit or a guarantee. Because of this, we are confident that when we die, we will go to Heaven and be with Him. As long as we are in this earthly body, including you who are reading this book, we are away from the LORD for now (even though HE is ALWAYS with us by His Spirit living in us). Yet right now, while we are still in these earthly bodies, we are not able to physically touch and hug Him. To keep it simple, He is up there, and we are still here—until finally we'll be in HEAVEN with HIM one glorious day. For now, we walk and live by faith and not by sight. We are confident and would rather be out of this earthly body and instead be in Heaven with our new bodies, with our LORD!

The Bible's view of receiving a new body is similar to changing clothes. Here is an example that I will share with you all concerning my dear mom's funeral some years ago. Even though my precious mom, Hazel Smiling, is no longer on this earth with us, I still am really joyfully happy for her sake, because she is no longer suffering with her older earthly body that at that point was causing her so much pain. Therefore, while we were in the funeral, I explained to the people there with us that inside my mom's casket was her old body. Her spirit had left that old body that was full of pain. Her spirit went to Heaven, and the LORD gave her spirit a new body to live in with HIM forever!

Here is an example that I have used, and you can also try to do it yourself. Go get a shirt or sweater, and let me know when you get back. Oh, you are back—great! That shirt represents your new body from Heaven. The one that you are wearing now represents your old body. Now, take off the shirt or sweater that you have on now, which represents the old body, and lay that "old body" on a chair or the floor, to be buried, so to speak. OK—now, put on the other shirt. The shirt you put on now represents your new body. Notice that you did not die? You simply changed clothes. That's what happens when our bodies die. Our natural body will die—perish, turn to dust—yet in an instant, in the twinkling of an eye, our spirits will be in our new bodies with GOD in HEAVEN! Yes, your spirit will be in Heaven, and in fact, you will not die at all—only your body will. You will just change bodies—from an earthly one to a new heavenly body. In CHRIST JESUS there IS ETERNAL LIFE. Our bodies will be changed from the old to the new ones! Awesome! GOD simply explained through His word in the Bible that we will be clothed so that we won't be found naked. GOD giving us a new body is as simple as changing clothes! Wow!

Some of you reading this book right now may be pastors or teachers, and if you would like, you can share this illustration with others using a black suit and a white suit jacket. The black suit jacket that you are wearing that day can represent your old body. The white suit jacket will represent your new body from Heaven. At my mom's funeral, I took the black jacket off and laid it on her casket, representing her old body. Then I put on the white jacket, representing her new body in Heaven. This visual has comforted many people over the years. It sheds a new light on "to be absent from the body is to be present with the LORD." Amen!

Never was this scripture passage truer than at the cross: "Absent from the body is to be present with LORD." Again, take your Bible and read Luke 23:39–47. But before you read, let me set the scene: The day that Jesus was crucified for my sin, your sin, and the sins of the world, He was hung on a cross. His cross was placed in the middle of two criminals also hanging on crosses. He had one criminal hanging to His right and one criminal hanging on His left. It was on a main road in Jerusalem, at the foot of mountain called the skull. I was there, visiting Israel this past summer, and we can still see this huge skull face, about the size of a head on Mount Rushmore. I am an eyewitness to the actual spot where JESUS was murdered for my sins and yours. I was in the actual garden where Jesus was betrayed. I have in my wallet olive leaves from the garden of Gethsemane. The place of the skull was on the side of the main road, just outside Jerusalem. The reason the Romans killed people on a main road was so that everyone could see and be afraid.

OK, you can begin reading Luke 23 now. For those of you reading this book on a train, plane, or bus, I hope you do have your Bible with you; if not, maybe you can download a free Bible app on your phone, tablet, or iPad. Here is the scripture:

> One of the criminals who hung there hurled insults at Him: "Aren't you the Christ? Save yourself and us!" But the other criminal rebuked him. "Don't you fear God," he said, "since you are under the same sentence? We are punished justly, for we are getting what our deeds deserve. But this man has done nothing wrong." Then he said, "Jesus, remember me when you come into your kingdom." Jesus answered him, "I tell you the truth, today you will be with Me in paradise." It was now about the sixth hour, and darkness came over the whole land until the ninth hour, for the sun stopped shining. And the temple curtain was torn in two. Jesus called out with a loud voice, "Father, into your hands I commit my spirit." When He said this, He breathed His last. The centurion, seeing what had happened, praised God and said, "Surely this was a righteous man."

OK, you may place your Bibles down now. I ask you to meditate on Jesus's reply to the converted criminal. "I tell you the truth, today you will be with me in paradise." Notice the words "the truth" and "today." Clearly CHRIST JESUS is stating what we already read, that to be absent from the body is to be present with the LORD! The criminal just wanted Jesus to remember him when He got to Heaven. Jesus, seeing that the criminal had had a change of heart, told the man that HE was taking him that very same day with HIM to Heaven—not tomorrow, not sleep in your grave first—but "today, you will be with Me in Paradise." Here is the point: your last breath on earth is your next breath in HEAVEN, with GOD! That is amazingly awesome! As you can see, the criminal repented in his last hours of life, and GOD had mercy on him. As soon as the converted criminal died, he went to Heaven and got his new body. GOD's MERCY is so GREAT, and it gives us great joy to know that when a believer's body dies, he or she goes to HEAVEN.

On the other hand, when a nonbeliever dies, he goes ahhh! Let's see what happens to a person who doesn't trust God—a nonbeliever. Take your Bible, and open it to Luke 16:19. Again, for those of you reading this book without your Bibles, here is the verse:

> There was a certain rich man, who was clothed in purple and fine linen, and fared sumptuously every day; and there was a certain beggar named Lazarus, which lay at the gate, full of sores, and desiring to be fed with crumbs which fell from the rich man's table; moreover, the dogs came and licked his sores. And it came to pass that the beggar died and was carried by the angels into Abram's bosom; the rich man died also, and was buried.

By the way, you can feel free to read a different translation of the Bible than the one I use, which is the old King James Version long before LeBron, if it helps you understand these scriptures better. You may use the New King James Version (NKJV), my NBA guys and girls, again not LeBron, the New International Version (NIV), or the New Living Translation, and/or the Message Bible, and so on.

OK, now I would like to point out a few things. Back to the scripture. The beggar Lazarus being taken to Abraham bosom was another way of saying that he was taken to Heaven, because that is the place where Abraham is. If you went to Heaven, and Abraham was to give you a hug, you would be in his bosom. He would put his arms around you, and your head would be in his bosom or another, for *bosom* means "chest," thus against his chest. When people generally hug each other, they do it with their arms and chest or bosom. Notice that when Lazarus the beggar died, GOD sent angels to carry him to Heaven. Also let me point to something very important in the verse: notice that Abraham is alive, not dead. Abraham is alive in Heaven, and so are all of the believers that left this earth and are in Heaven. As I have been saying throughout this book, HEAVEN is a REAL PLACE, and everyone there is ALIVE and BETTER than they ever were here on earth.

In the other hand, when the rich man—a nonbeliever—died and was buried, here is what happened to him:

> And in hell he lifted up his eyes, being in torment, and sees Abraham afar off and Lazarus in his bosom. And he cried and said, "Father Abraham, have mercy on me, and send Lazarus that he may dip the tip of his finger in water and cool my tongue, for I am tormented in this flame." But Abraham said, "Son, remember that thou in thy lifetime received thy good things, and likewise, Lazarus, evil things; but now he is comforted, and thou art tormented.(Luke 16:23)

Let's pause for a moment. Here, as you can see, the people in hell can also see, hear, feel, touch—and REMEMBER! In hell, people will be able to see the beauty and splendor of Heaven yet be constantly tormented in flames, forever regretting the fact that they rejected the salvation of the LORD JESUS CHRIST. They are in torment, crying out for mercy every day as the pain of the fire constantly burns their bodies forever. They can REMEMBER every time they heard the Gospel (the good news of CHRIST), and they said, "That's not for me. I am a good person," and because of their rejecting the TRUTH of the

LORD that could have saved them, they now will suffer forever. GOD makes it very clear in the BIBLE that HE does not want people to suffer in hell, so HE gives them the CHOICE now, while they are alive here on earth, for them to call on HIM, asking for forgiveness and repenting from their evil works, turning away from wrongdoing, and asking CHRIST JESUS to SAVE their souls.

By the way, if you still have not made a decision for CHRIST, please do so now, for your own sake. You don't want to wind up in hell even after reading the encouragements and warnings in this book. That's just crazy! The suffering and pain that humans sometimes suffer in this earth is nothing in comparison to the suffering and pain that will be in hell. Since they will be forever away from GOD's presence, the suffering will be horrible forever! This is not like getting burned on stove or an iron! It's going to be twenty-four hours a day, seven days a week—nonstop suffering and pain! Flames and pain all over your entire body that you can see, hear, smell, taste, and touch. My prayer is that you would CHOOSE LIFE, choose CHRIST. If you choose HIM and HIS LOVE, then in HEAVEN you will be, together with everyone else who chose to BELIEVE— how BEAUTIFUL it will be! With the LORD, you will escape the suffering that was never meant for you.

For those who still don't want to repent, don't be fooled. Just because things are going your way now, and things are going well for you here on earth, it does not mean that you're right with GOD. The rich man had everything in his life here on earth—he seemed to be blessed of God and highly favored! Lazarus, on the other hand, had a terrible life of suffering, and one would question God's love for him. For those who are going through a very hard time and suffering now while here on earth, that does not mean that GOD is angry at you. No, He is not angry at you. This world is not perfect; sometimes there will be pain and suffering. Yet if you call on the LORD, HE will comfort you, strengthen you, and give you HIS PEACE, and maybe He will get you out of the situation you are in. If not, all the more reason to look forward to going to Heaven at whatever time He chooses for us to go there with HIM and out of this crazy world.

OK—now, here's a little more explanation on the rich man that had a great life but was not right with God and therefore went to hell. The rich man didn't go to hell because he was rich. Being rich is a good thing—if the riches are shared with people who are in need. Being rich can be such a big blessing if used in a balanced way, helping others along with helping yourself. The LORD commands us through HIS word that we are to LOVE one another as we love ourselves. Therefore, riches in themselves can be used as Blessings; however, this particular rich man that the LORD speaks about in the Bible never gave the poor beggar anything. He did not share with him or help him in any way. There was no help for Lazarus from the rich man, even though things got so bad for poor Lazarus that he just wanted the crumbs from the rich man's table to eat. But through it all, this Lazarus had a relationship with GOD, and in the end, HE got the Greatest Reward—arriving in Heaven. There is more to explain, but since this is a book about Heaven and not hell, we will stop here concerning that topic. You can read the rest on your own—it may be found in Luke 16:19–31. And know this—it is appointed to a man once to die and then the judgment. You will either spend eternity in Heaven with our HEAVENLY FATHER GOD or in hell, tormented forever while burning in the lake of fire. The choice is up to you.

With GOD, you will never be alone, and even when your earthly body dies, your spirit and soul will never die. As soon as one of GOD's children dies, He sends His angels to come and get them and take them to Heaven. Again, going back to Luke 19:22: "The time came when the beggar Lazarus died, and angels carried him to Abraham's bosom." GOD Himself is also described as the angel of the LORD in Psalms 23: "Yea, though I walk through the valley of the shadow of death, I will fear no evil: for thou art with me; thy rod and thy staff, they comfort me." That's why sometimes you will see loved ones looking up just before they die. Some of them have huge smiles on their faces before they exit this earth to then enter into Heaven. At that moment, they can see the angels coming.

I will never forget when my first wife, Laverne, went home to be with the LORD. I was rushing her to Jamaica Hospital Medical Center. She couldn't breathe because of an asthma attack. My oldest son was sitting in the backseat of our vehicle. He was eight years old at the time. Just before we got off the expressway, she took her last breath. When she took her last breath, the car was filled with the presence of GOD and angels. I could not see them, but I could definitely feel them. Right after that brief moment, just like that, she was gone. I was left with her old body, for the angels took her spirit to get her new body in Heaven from GOD, a body not made with human hands.

Genesis 2:24 says "Therefore shall a man leave his father and mother, and cleave unto his wife: and they shall be one flesh." Because she and I were one flesh in marriage, when her earthly body died, I remember that I could sense the tearing and ripping of our souls apart as she left. I felt a physical pain in my heart as if it were being sliced in half. It was so profound—it felt physical, yet I wasn't even touched! It hurt so much that for weeks, months, I thought I was going to die. It wasn't until I began to study the word of GOD that I could finally understand what had happened that day. The two of us had been one, and one of us was torn away at death, when angels carried my dear Laverne into Heaven. Now I can actually rejoice, being really happy for her, because she is in the BEST PLACE anyone can ever be—HEAVEN. At that time, however, I did not understand all this, that Laverne had left me with her old body and went to Heaven and got her new body. Also, at the time I didn't know that GOD could raise the dead and that there was life after death. I was angry, because I thought Laverne was lost forever. We had been childhood sweethearts, together since she was fourteen years of age and I was thirteen—and then at age thirty-two, she was gone! Imagine the anger and the pain that I felt, since I thought that she was gone forever!

But now that I know HEAVEN is a REAL PLACE, imagine what great JOY and peace I have! I realize that Laverne got the best deal of all. She is in the best circumstances right now—with GOD in Heaven, never to die again! She went to Heaven at a young age, and at the time, I thought it was the worst thing. However, she was young when she went to GOD that early, so she did not have to suffer the extra struggles of a longer life. She was still young and very beautiful. She got to live on earth a year less than Jesus did. He was thirty-three years of age when He gave His life for us all, and she was thirty-two when she went to her heavenly home to be with Him. She was always a stunningly beautiful woman, inside and out, and now she is perfect, forever! And it's really awesome to know that she is there with some of your family members and friends who are already in Heaven now, along with my mom also and, best of all, with GOD and the LORD JESUS CHRIST! One great and glorious day, we will see them again. Awesome! In the meantime, while we are here on earth, GOD gives us the strength to live unto His purpose for our lives. After Laverne went home with the LORD, I was able to go on with life and years later get married again. I am blessed with my wonderful and very beautiful wife, Neyra, two sons, and twin daughters! GLORY to GOD!

As I continue to write this book, different events keep happening in this world, some of which I will write about in hopes of encouraging you with truth in the midst of it all. Today is March 11, 2011, and an earthquake with a magnitude of 8.9 just hit Japan. The earthquake caused a tsunami, and waves of water over twenty-three feet high swept through the city. So far, many precious people's lives are gone. We do pray and ask GOD to comfort the families they represent, and even in the midst of this, the reality is that over seventeen thousand lives are either with CHRIST the LORD in Heaven. Or, some may be in hell, waiting for the lake of fire. Only GOD knows. That number is increasing even as I am writing this book. Some of those thousands of precious people are filled with joy in Heaven right now, and they will never suffer again. The others are suffering now and will continue to burn forever. For some, Heaven is a real place. For others, hell is a real place. Out of this horrible, horrible tragedy, for some it is the best day of their lives. For others, it is the worst day of their lives. If they have not made their peace with GOD, hell will be a lot worse. GOD perhaps took with Him some of the people that cried, "Oh GOD, please help me!" But some won't even say that, because "a fool has said in his heart that there is no God." To them, this is a very sad day indeed.

Fast forward in time—today is July 16, 2016, and I am proofreading this book for the final time before I hand it over to be published. Donald Trump and Hillary Clinton are running for president of the United States, and things in this world are getting worse. In Nice, France, a truck driver ran over and killed eighty-four innocent people. In Orlando, Florida, forty-nine people were killed at a club. Dallas shootings! ISIS! I pray for the families that are left behind. I write all this so that you can see that this is a book for now, for the times we live in! Like this November, when we choose a new president of the United States, you need to choose to be united with God—today, right now!

In the next chapter, "Wanted in Heaven, Dead or Alive," we will talk about going to Heaven alive. But before we go there, dear reader, where are you now spiritually? Are you sure you are going to Heaven? How about your family and friends? Are they friends of GOD or enemies of GOD? Is JESUS CHRIST their LORD? Or is Satan their lord? If you've already made your peace with GOD, I strongly encourage you to keep praying for your family and friends. I may not be able to reach them now, but you can. Share GOD's LOVE with them and encourage them to the LORD's TRUTH. I pray that you understand that you are reading this book by divine appointment. Someone may have given you this book. You may have bought it yourself. Maybe you are reading it in the library or perhaps on line, on your phone, iPad, or tablet. However, it is GOD Who made sure you get this book. He did so because He loves you, and He desires to bless and save you! Not only you, because after you believe, you can share the truth with others so that they too may be saved. The LORD is able to save them from whatever it is they need saving from right now. Your helping them toward the truth can save them from going to hell and being separated from GOD forever! Being in hell and separated from the LORD is far worse than any earthquake! The question again is, where are you spiritually? Run to the LORD, stay close to HIM, and be encouraged to help guide others to draw near to GOD.

CHAPTER 4

Wanted in Heaven, Dead or Alive

For those of you who are still afraid to die, here is some great news. You don't have to die to go to Heaven. GOD can take you there alive. Heaven is the land of the living. Remember I mentioned before that some of us will not see death and will be taken into Heaven alive? It will happen in an instant. Also know that in the last days, just before the end of the world, GOD is going to destroy this sinful world—the earth, the sun, the moon, and the stars—all of it. And HE will create a new world without sin. Yes, it's true—there will be no sin there at all. No evil can stand in the LORD's presence, for HE is HOLY and ALMIGHTY, and none is greater than HE—none. We will live with GOD on the new earth in the new city of Jerusalem. Even as I am writing this book, I think I may include toward the end a chapter concerning the last day. But in the meantime, let's continue learning about going to Heaven alive. Heaven is the land of the living. Throughout the Bible, from the Old Testament to the New (that is, from Genesis to Revelation), we read about how GOD has taken people to Heaven alive. Some people, like Enoch, went to Heaven alive and did not come back. Another from the Old Testament who did not die but went to Heaven alive is the prophet Elijah, who was taken up in a fiery chariot. In the New Testament, the apostle Paul and John the Beloved are written about, both of whom went to Heaven and came back to write about it.

Let's start from the beginning. What I am going to do now is quickly move through the Bible from Genesis to Revelation. In this process, we will look through the scriptures for those who went to Heaven alive. Try to have your Bible handy. If you do not, it's OK; I will give you the scripture. As before, I will quote the scripture, providing chapter and verse, and then I will explain what we are reading.

First, let's recap who is in Heaven so far, according to the earlier scriptures also mentioned in this book. GOD, the LORD JESUS is in Heaven. Abraham and Lazarus the beggar are there too. The host of angels that took Lazarus to Heaven is there also, and even the thief on the cross. By the way, knowing about the thief on the cross really blesses me. He represents so many people, even some of our loved ones, who at the last moments of their lives had a change of heart—and CHRIST the LORD took them. The thief on the cross He took to Heaven that very same day! That may be one of the reasons why the Bible says that the first shall be last, and the last shall be first.

There will be many surprises when we get to Heaven. Some people will be there in Heaven with us that you and I thought would never make it. And concerning others, we will be stunned that they *didn't* make it. Some will be very surprised to see you and me there, and others knew all along that we would be there. Here are some of the scriptures about the people who went to Heaven alive and are living there to this day and unto eternity.

Genesis 5:24: "And Enoch walked with GOD: and he was not, for GOD took him." By faith, Enoch was taken to Heaven that he should not see death, and he was not found because GOD took him—for before this, he walked with GOD throughout his life and had a testimony that pleased GOD. How great and amazing it is that the LORD took him to Heaven alive! Let that sink into your mind, heart, and spirit. Pause for a moment, receive revelation from GOD, and allow HIS HOLY SPIRIT to breathe life into your understanding of this. Enoch lived a life so pleasing to God that the Lord took him straight to Heaven without Enoch's having to die! Wow! No offence, Star Trek fans, but that's really a "beam me up, Scotty"! HEAVEN is a REAL PLACE with living people, not ghosts, not just spirits. There are real live people like you and me but even BETTER, because they are PERFECT and are in a PERFECT PLACE with a PERFECT GOD! By the way, they found some of Enoch's writings in Ethiopia. You can go online and read the book of Enoch for yourself. He was a real man that GOD took to Heaven alive.

In your Bible, turn to 2 Kings 2:1–11 in the Old Testament. "Then it happened, as they continued and talked, that suddenly a chariot of fire appeared with horses of fire and separated the two of them; and Elijah went up by a whirlwind into Heaven." OK, here you have Elijah the prophet walking along the Jordan River with his servant Elisha. If you study your Bible, you'll realize that Elisha became the next prophet after Elijah went to Heaven. In fact, Elijah told him that the only way he could get a double portion of his power was to see him go into Heaven. Needless to say, Elisha stayed close to Elijah until they were separated by the chariot of fire and Elijah was taken into Heaven. Fifty sons of the prophets watching from a distance saw when it happened, so altogether there were fifty-one people who saw Elijah going into Heaven alive, riding the chariot of fire, with horses of fire on top of a tornado! Look again at verse 7, which reads: "And fifty men of sons of the prophets went and stood facing them at a distance while the two of them stood by the Jordan River."

I have a picture that I took while I was in Israel of a statue built to honor Elijah. The statue was built on the very spot where Elijah called down fire from Heaven. These were real men and real events with eye witnesses. In a court of law, one eyewitness is enough for a jury to put a person away for life. Fifty-one witnesses are more than enough. In the New Testament, when John wrote the book of Revelation, he went to Heaven:

> After this, I looked and behold, a door was opened in Heaven: and the first voice which I heard was as if it were of a trumpet talking to me; which said come up hither, and I will show you things which must be hereafter. And immediately I was in the spirit: and behold, a throne was set in Heaven, and one that sat on the throne. (Rev. 4:1–2)

John was in the throne room with JESUS the CHRIST. "And He that sat was to look upon like jasper and sardine stone: and there was a rainbow round about the throne, in sight like unto an emerald." (Rev. 4:3)

Paul was another who also went to Heaven, but he was told not to tell anybody what he saw or heard. Heaven was so real that it almost blew Paul's mind.

> I knew a man in Christ above fourteen years ago, whether in the body, I cannot tell or whether out of the body, I cannot tell;

36

God knoweth; such a one was caught up to the Third Heaven. And I knew such a man (whether in the body or out of the body, I cannot tell; God knoweth; how that he was caught up onto paradise and heard unspeakable words which it is not lawful for a man to utter. (2 Cor. 12:2–4)

Heaven is so awesome and so beautiful that Paul was speechless! Paul wasn't sure if he'd gone to Heaven in his earthly body or if he'd had what we call today an out-of-body experience. You may want know what Paul saw, right? I will share more on that, but we still have some unfinished business in this chapter. I named this chapter "Wanted in Heaven, Dead or Alive" to help take the sting out of death. God loves you very much, and when you are done down here, He wants you to be with Him forever! It doesn't matter how you get there, by death or like Enoch, but GOD can take you up alive. Just get there! God has issued a love warrant for you! You are wanted in Heaven, dead or alive!

In the next few verses, I will show you two men, both alive and talking to Jesus. One died and went to Heaven; the other, as we just read, went to Heaven alive. Both men are now back from Heaven, alive and talking to Jesus during His transfiguration. One of men, Moses, had died, and his body was taken to Heaven. The other man, Elijah, as you just read, went to Heaven in the most spectacular manner—in a chariot of fire, horses of fire, and a whirlwind! Wow! If you have seen the movie *The Ten Commandments*, you remember that Charlton Heston played Moses and that Yul Brynner played Pharaoh Ramses II. The main man I want to focus on now is Moses.

Moses died after finishing all of his work for the LORD GOD. If you have been reading this book from the beginning, the question I have for you is, did Moses really die? Here is the answer, starting with Deuteronomy 34:4–6: "And the LORD said to him, this is the land which I swore unto Abraham, unto Isaac, and unto Jacob, saying I will give it unto thy seed: I have caused thee to see it with thine eyes, but thou shall not go thither." So, Moses, the servant of the Lord, died there in the land of Moab according to the word of the Lord. And GOD buried him in a valley in the land of Moab over against Beth-peor. But no man knows of his sepulchre, not even today. OK, that was simple enough—Moses died just like GOD said he would. HE buried him in an unknown grave, right?

In fact, Joshua 1:1–2 says:

> Now after the death of Moses, the servant of the Lord, it came to pass that the Lord spoke unto Joshua, the son of Nun, Moses's minister, saying, "Moses my servant is dead; now therefore arise, go over this Jordan, thou and this entire people, unto the land which I do give them, even to the children of Israel."

So, Moses is dead, right? No, not so fast. But before I go on, there are two things I want you to keep in mind. Moses (as we just read) is dead, and Elijah (as we all know) went to Heaven alive. Now, let's continue on. I want to fast-forward to the Lord Jesus and the transfiguration. For those of you who might not know, Jesus took Peter, John, and James up on a mountain to pray. We call it the transfiguration because Jesus was changed into His glory from Heaven. Read Luke 9:28–36. For those of you without your Bible handy, I will start at verse 28: "And it came to pass about eight days after these sayings, He took Peter and John and James, and went up into a mountain to pray. And as He prayed, the fashion of His countenance was altered, and His raiment was white and glistering." OK, here you have JESUS transforming into heavenly glory. He was glowing in His glory to the point that His clothes were even changed and glistering white. Ever seen lightning? JESUS was brighter than that!

Now, the next verse is one of the reasons I asked you to receive the Holy Spirit. You need GOD's help so that you will be able to understand what you are about to read. Just a simple prayer will do: "LORD, help me to understand what I am about to read." Go ahead—pray before you read any more. I will wait here

Praise the LORD for those of you who prayed! For those of you who didn't, I suggest you skip the rest of this chapter and go to the next chapter, "Heaven Is a Real Place"; it will be a little easier to understand. For the rest of us, here are verses 30–31: "And, behold, there talked with Him two men, which were Moses and Elijah, who appeared in glory, and spoke of His decease, which He should accomplish at Jerusalem." Hold on! I thought we just read that Moses was dead. But here he is, alive and talking to Jesus and Elijah. And this was not a dream. Look at verses 32–36:

> But Peter and they that were with him were heavy with sleep: and when they were awake, they saw His glory, and the two men that stood with Him. And it came to pass, as they departed from Him, Peter said unto Jesus, "Master, it is good for us to be here: and let us make three tabernacles; one for Thee and one for Moses, and one for Elijah: not knowing what he had said." While he thus spoke, there came a cloud, and overshadowed them: and they feared as they entered into the cloud. And there came a voice out of the cloud, saying, "This is My beloved Son: hear Him. And when the voice was past, Jesus was found alone. And they kept close, and told no man in those days any of those things which they had seen.

OK, sit back and think about what you just read. This scripture is the foundation for this entire book. When the Lord opened my eyes to this, I knew I had to write a book about Heaven being a real place, a land of the living. Here we have Jesus talking to the two men from Heaven. One died and went to Heaven. The other took the express bus to Heaven, so to speak—Elijah went by chariot of fire and a tornado. Moses died, and his old body was buried by God in an unknown grave, and his spirit body was taken to Heaven by the archangel Michael. There, God gave him his new body. For you Bible scholars, here is the verse. Jude 1:9: "Yet Michael the archangel, when contending with the devil he disputed about the body of Moses, durst not bring against him a railing accusation but said, 'The Lord rebuke thee.'"

Again, you are wanted in Heaven, dead or alive. As I said before, your last breath on earth is your next breath in Heaven. It happens so fast, in the twinkling of an eye—not even a full blink! Michael carried Moses into Heaven so fast that we have no words here on earth to describe it. But as you read before, the key is that you don't die—you step out of your old body and into the new. Notice that both men appeared in their new, glorified bodies. Luke 9, the end of verses 30–31: "Which were Moses and Elijah, who appeared in glory."

Give me a second while I take a praise break! OK, thanks. I am back. You see, Jesus put on glory to talk to glory. I love the genius of God in making sure you know that this was no dream but a real, live happening. The Bible says in verse 32: "But Peter and they that were with Him were heavy with sleep: and when they were awake, they saw His glory, and the two men that stood with Him." These men were in their new bodies not made with human hands but by God from Heaven. And notice that Peter was able to recognize them. He called them by name. When you see your family members in Heaven, you will be able to recognize them for sure, and they will know you. There is so much here to share that I would have to write another book, but for the sake of this one, let's stay on course.

So again, Heaven is a real place. People in Heaven are alive and not resting in the grave, for they are in Heaven. That's why God put the transfiguration in the Bible. One, to confirm Jesus as the only Lord God and perfect sacrifice. "This is my beloved son, hear Him." Two, so that we can see that Heaven is a real place with live human beings. Three, to show that if you put your trust in Him, you never really die. Only your outer body does. The real you, your soul and spirit, will leave this body, go to Heaven, and then be clothed with a new one. That's why He sent Moses back with Elijah. He could have sent Enoch. Remember, He loved Enoch so much that He just took him. No, He sent Moses, representing our family and friends that have died. That's because the truth is that we never die—we just change the old, imperfect body for a new body that is perfect and will never perish. That's why Jesus says that you HAVE eternal life. Think about it. Why do you think life with God is called everlasting life? Your body dies, but you don't. If you died, even for one second, it could not be called everlasting life.

Let's recap. Moses left his body, went to Heaven, and got a new one that will never die. Elijah went to Heaven in his old body, and God changed him into his new body that will never die. Jesus isn't sitting on the throne in Heaven by Himself, people. Wake up! Eternal life means eternal life. Everlasting life means exactly that—EVERLASTING LIFE! If you died, it wouldn't mean that you live forever, now would it? Duh! Mary is there, John is there, angels are there, my mom, your grandmomma, Dr. King—so many others are already there! Touch two people around you and say, "Grandma was right!" "The nuns were right!" "My pastor was right!—Jesus is the truth!"

> Wherefore seeing we also are compassed about with so great a cloud of witnesses, let us lay aside every weight and the sin which doth so easily beset us, and let us run with patience the race that is set before us. Looking unto Jesus, the Author and Finisher of our faith, who for the joy that was set before Him endured the cross, despising the shame, and is set down at the right hand of the throne of God.

The people in Heaven can come down and have dinner with us if God were to let them. But who would want to leave Heaven? But that is exactly what happened! The Lord and two angels came down from Heaven and had dinner with Abraham.

In Genesis 18, the LORD came down from Heaven with two angels to tell Abraham that Sarah was going to have a baby. While they were there, Abraham made them a tender roasted calf. I am not sure if Sarah was a good cook or not, but when I see her in Heaven, I may ask her! I am just kidding, Sister Sarah! These were the same two angels that GOD sent to destroy Sodom. The angels were so handsome that the people of Sodom wanted them for their ungodly pleasure. That was one of the many reasons why HE destroyed Sodom. But that's a story for another day. I just want you to see that people from Heaven can actually eat, just like you and I can. In fact, if an angel walked over to ask you for directions, you would not be able to tell he was an angel.

Open your Bible to Genesis 18:1–8. This will be the last scripture for this chapter, because I want to move on to the next chapter, "Heaven Is a Real Place." OK, Genesis 18:1–8 says:

> And the Lord appeared unto him in the plains of Mamre. And Abraham lifted up his eyes and looked, and lo, three men stood

by him, and he said, "My Lord, if now I have found favor in Thy sight, please; now let a little water be fetched, wash Your feet, and rest. I will get You a morsel of bread so that You can refresh Your heart." Abraham hurried into the tent to Sarah and said, "Quickly, get three measures of fine flour, knead it, and bake bread." Then Abraham ran to the herd and fetched a tender and good calf. He took buttermilk and the calf which he had dressed, and set it before them. He stood by them under the tree, and they ate.

As you can see, the Lord from Heaven and two angels sat down and had a meal with Abraham. As I said, if an angel from Heaven were to walk over to you and have a brief conversation with you, you may never know an angel was speaking to you. In fact, when some of you have entertained strangers, you have entertained angels unaware.

This concludes the chapter, "Wanted in Heaven, Dead or Alive." I know that for some of you new believers, this was deep. For you nonbelievers, I am glad you stuck with it so far and are hanging in there. If you have been reading this book all the way through to this point, put it down and take a break. This has been real soul food that your soul and spirit needs to digest. I suggest that you think, meditate, and recheck your Bible notes before moving to the next chapter. I would rather that you pray about what you just read so that you get more revelation from the LORD. Again, this is the real soul food. Then, move on to the rest of the book, which is not as hard and much easier to read. The hard part is done; the foundation is set. Next stop, Heaven. Heaven is a real place.

CHAPTER 5

HEAVEN is a REAL PLACE

We are finally here, my beloved—Heaven! After four chapters of faith building, deaths, and resurrections, we are finally at the place where we all want to be. Everyone wants to go to Heaven, right? We went from the earth to the clouds to the moon and now, imagine, into Heaven's door. No more knocking on Heaven's door. It's time to go inside and see what life is like on the inside. This is the place many of us have looked forward to and dreamed about. Who is here? What does it look like? Are there homes here? Are there really streets paved with gold? Is there really a book of life? Am I in the book of life? What about the twenty-four elders—are they here?

Remember when I mentioned my friend the firefighter that was in the twin towers when they came down? I wrote that he'd never came out. However, GOD reminded me through my sister Josie, who is cowriting this book (Hi, Josie!), that my friend Benny did come out, and I have to clear that up. His old body did not come out. But his spirit went to Heaven, and Jesus put Benny into his new body! Praise GOD! Yes, he is in Heaven alive! Not only Benny but also every person in those towers who belonged to GOD. God is here in Heaven, and all those who put their trust in Him are here! Those who have cried out for God during their last breaths are also here. Exactly who is here, only God knows. God LOVES all, and He is the One with the ability to see and read the heart of each person. He knows those who are His. It is also exciting to know that every one of you who gave your life to the LORD earlier while reading this book has everlasting life right now, so your names are written in the Lamb's book of life. In the meantime, while on earth, be encouraged to aim to live a godly life and please the LORD. Some People who are in heaven now are there because they lived a life that was pleasing to the Lord Jesus. Some lived for God all of their lives, and others got it right at the last second, like the thief on the cross. So, those of you with loved ones who have gone on, don't judge; instead, dream of meeting them in Heaven. Only God knows if they are there, and we will find out when we get there.

In chapter 8 of this book, "The Last Day," I will let you know more about what type of people definitely won't make it to Heaven. I'll give you a hint: it has to do with a hard heart and repentance. Please don't turn to that chapter yet. You might know someone who fits that description, and it may lead you to misjudge someone ahead of time. And as I stated before, only GOD knows who will eventually turn to HIM or not. You'll find many surprises when you get there. Some will be shocked that you made it, LOL! He is the only righteous judge able to see inside our hearts, our minds, and our souls. He knows our motives—and our heart.

OK, back to Heaven. You made it! You are in Heaven now! There are no more tears, no more sickness, no more suffering, and no more death. Every baby that was ever aborted is alive and at the perfect age that God wanted the child to live at in the first place. Everyone has perfect vision, so there's no need for glasses. Everyone has arms and legs, and so on. Everyone is perfect! We are perfect in the way we look and perfect in our love for GOD and each other. There's no jealousy, no false motives, no lies, and no deceit. Here, there is nothing to lie about. Everything here is true and perfect. Just think—no wrinkles, no overweight, and no underweight. We will have perfect eyes, hair color, nails, and muscles—perfect! Here, your mind is brilliant and perfect—no more forgetting anything. Just think, your entire being—body, mind, soul, and spirit— will be perfect, the way GOD intended it to be. Heaven is completely perfect! The most beautiful flowers you have ever seen, you will see. Everything is new, with a newness that will last forever.

We really cannot comprehend how beautiful Heaven is because the world we live in is so imperfect, but try your best to think and meditate. Look at some old photos of yourself when you looked and felt your best, and multiply that by a billon, because in Heaven you will look and feel better than that! Everything that you don't like about yourself and others will be gone forever! The people of the Bible, like Abraham, Isaac, and Jacob, are all here. We will also see Dr. King; he really is free at last. Picture your old buddies from high school—they are here. My older brother's son is here—my nephew. He only lived for a day or so on earth. Now, he is at the perfect age that the LORD had set for him.

I want you to fill in the blanks and have your own wonderful ideas of who may be here. They are all in Heaven and perfect, as God wanted them to be. They know you, and you know them. You loved them, and you missed them before, but now you are no longer in sorrow because they are here with GOD, alive like never before. And the love you feel here is indescribable. There's so much joy and so much peace. There are no more time limits or constraints, for there are no clocks or watches in Heaven. No need for cars or trucks; you just think about where you want to go, and you are there. No need for phones; we are connected to each other now by the HOLY SPIRIT.

Think about what we just read. Remember Moses and Elijah? Since Heaven is so far away that we cannot measure it, they would have had to travel at instant speed. In Heaven, we all have the same type of body that JESUS has. How do I know? The answer is in 1 John 3:2: "Beloved, now we are the sons of GOD, and it does not yet appear what we shall be: but we know that when He shall appear, we shall be like Him; for we shall see Him as He is." We shall be like Him. In Heaven, you are with CHRIST, and you shall be like Him! In the trans-figuration, when the LORD was talking to Elijah and Moses, who were in their glorified bodies, JESUS showed forth His glory also. In Acts 1, Christ Jesus also ascended to Heaven as the disciples watched. During the ascension, Jesus traveled up toward Heaven at a slow speed, and then a cloud hid Him. He went up slowly so that people could see Him going into Heaven. Once out of our sight, He was in Heaven in an instant. Jesus traveled at a speed not known here on earth. To us, it is fast; to Jesus not so much. We all will travel at the same speed in Heaven. It's like instant speed—the heavenly body is able to just appear out of nowhere. Remember when the disciples were behind closed doors? Jesus just appeared. On earth, we don't have anything to measure the speed of God or God's people.

God, unlike the rest of us, is not a respecter of persons. In Heaven, He gives us all the same capabilities. He loves us all the same. The chariot that Elijah rode into Heaven was for our benefit, so that we could remember and read about it today and understand that Heaven is alive, filled with living people. As you can see, when Elijah and Moses came back to talk to Jesus, no chariot was needed. They just appeared. We will not need the space shuttle; I can just visit Mars on my own! Ha-ha-ha! There will be a new LA, a new France, and new New York, and so on. God is going to remake the entire Heavens and earth. Like the great master builder, He will destroy this world and make all things new. He intends to make everything perfect, the way it was in the beginning.

If you have read this book up to this point and still have doubts, keep it simple: if GOD did it once, He can do it again. "With God, nothing is impossible!" He made this earth, and He can make a new one!

For all you readers, if you buy this book for someone, please encourage them to have a Bible handy. I would rather for them to be able to read these things for themselves. And for those of you that are having someone else read this to you, know that you too will be very blessed upon hearing everything here. May the LORD bless you all richly. Those who can read and research on their own I would like to cross-reference, to check what they just read in their own Bibles. They may see something that I missed. I want them to have the right perception of Heaven, for precept must be upon precept, line upon line, line upon line, here a little, and there a little.

Now, turn in your Bible to John 14:1—4:

> Let not your heart be troubled; ye believe in God, believe also in Me. In My Father's house are many mansions, abodes; if it were not so, I would have told you. I go to prepare a place for you. And if I go and prepare a place for you, I will come again, and receive you unto myself; that where I am, there ye may be also. And where I go, you know, and the way you know.

Here we can see that in Heaven, there are mansions or abodes. What Jesus is saying is that in Heaven, you will have your own place to live. Remember what Jesus said to Peter when Peter said, "Lord, we have left everything to follow You"? Jesus answered:

> Verily I say unto you, there is no man that hath left house, or
> brethren, or sisters, or father, or mother, or wife, or children,
> or lands, for My sake, and the Gospels, but he shall receive a
> hundredfold now in this time, houses, and brethren, and sis-
> ters, and mothers, and children and lands with persecutions;
> and in the world to come eternal life.

Here, we realize that what you will receive in Heaven will be at least a hundred times better than what's here on earth—lands, homes, and eternal life! Some may think that all one does in Heaven is stay at the temple and worship Jesus. But you will have your own place to go to also. There will be things to do, kingdoms to visit, places to go, people to meet. "In My Father's house there are many abodes." Think about all the people who are already there in Heaven, from Adam and Eve up to today. Think about we who are still here waiting to go to Heaven and about all those that will be saved in the near future. GOD will make a new Heaven and a new earth.

But let's continue to concentrate on Heaven today. (Now, there's a name for a new talk show—*Heaven Today!*) OK, moving right along! The name of the city in which all the people in Heaven are living today is called New Jerusalem. This is where our loved ones are today. Keeping it simple, it's as if GOD would say, "I used men to build the old city Jerusalem, but the heavenly city Jerusalem I will build Myself." Your Jerusalem now is a reminder of the greater one to come. Remember that this book is a series of connecting the dots. God wants you to take what you can see and connect it to what you cannot see. Look at Revelation 21:1–3:

> Then I saw a new Heaven and a new earth, for the first Heaven
> and the first earth had passed away, and there was no longer
> any sea. I saw the holy city, the New Jerusalem, coming down
> out of Heaven from GOD, prepared as a bride, beautifully
> dressed for her husband. And I heard a loud voice from the
> throne saying, "Now the dwelling of God is with men, and He
> will live with them. They will be His people, and God Himself
> will be with them and be their God."

OK, there is a lot here, but let me break it down for you. For those of you reading the Bible for the first time, the book of Revelation is the revelation of Jesus Christ, which Jesus gave to John to show His servants what must soon take place. He made it known by sending His angel to His servant John, who testifies to everything he saw—that is, the word of God and the testimony of Jesus Christ. In the book of Revelation, John reveals things that he saw then and things that will happen in the near future.

Keeping this in mind, let's look again at Revelation 21:1. John said that he saw the new Heaven and the new earth, for the old had passed. This hasn't happen yet, as you well know, because we are still living on the old earth today, so these are things that will come to pass, and only GOD HIMSELF knows the day and the hour. As I told you before, God is going to destroy this world and make a new one. But look closely at what John says about the New Jerusalem. Revelation 21:2: "I saw the holy city, the New Jerusalem, coming down out of Heaven from God, prepared as a bride, beautifully dressed for her husband." Notice he said that he saw the New Jerusalem coming down—from where? Heaven! John saw the new city coming down from Heaven. That is Heaven today. That is where New Jerusalem is. That is where Jesus sits on the throne as God. That is where all our family is today. Jesus let John see the place that He had prepared, coming down from Heaven so that we could believe. Jesus didn't have to let John see the city coming down out of Heaven. He could have let John see the new Heaven and the new earth with New Jerusalem sitting in the new earth. But He let John see the New Jerusalem "coming out of Heaven" because that is where it is today. Remember the Third Heaven, paradise, where God is perfect. The New Jerusalem where GOD dwells is ALREADY PERFECT right now. However, the First and Second Heavens, the ones JESUS is going to make all over again, are still here where we live. Remember that the earth, the clouds, our solar system, galaxies, universe, and so on are called the First and Second Heavens. The Third Heaven, which is way above, so far away that we have nothing on earth that can help us see it or get to it, is the home of God. The New Jerusalem.

For those of you jumping ahead, this is not the book for that. I suggest that you go back and read from the beginning, and then this will make sense. The rest of us can move on. Verse 21:3: "And I heard a loud voice from the throne saying, 'Now the dwelling of God is with men, and He will live with them. They will be His people, and God Himself will be with them, and He will be their God.'" This is true today, and will be in the near future. JESUS dwells with the people of GOD in Heaven today. He also dwells inside every Christian believer today.

When Jesus makes the new earth, He will live in the New Jerusalem on the new earth, with His people. The New Jerusalem is so beautiful that John compared it to a bride on her wedding day. Many of us have seen a bride on her wedding day: so beautiful, so new, with beautiful hair, eyes, toes, nails—every detail down to her undergarments is perfect. On our wedding day, my wife, Neyra, looked so beautiful coming down the aisle of Highland Church that I almost fainted. The freshness of new love, a new start—come on, those of you who are married men! I am sure you understand what I mean! And to you married ladies, do you remember your flowers? Remember the awe of the crowd as the little flower girl and the little ring bearer passed? Ah, how beautiful...like the statement that says, "Something old, something new, something borrowed, something blue."

However, in Heaven, nothing is old, nothing is borrowed, and all things are NEW. LOVE is new forever. Heaven is new forever! Forever means forever with JESUS! Awesome! No tears! No pain!

> "And Jesus shall wipe away all tears from your eyes; and there shall be no more death, neither sorrow, nor crying; neither shall there be any more pain, for the former things are passed away." And Jesus said, "Behold, I make all things new." And He said unto me, "Write, for these words are true and faithful." And He said unto me, "It is done. I am the Alpha and Omega, the beginning and the end. I will give of the fountain of the water of life freely to him who thirsts. He that overcometh shall inherit all things, and I will be his God, and he shall be My son." (Rev. 21:4–7)

Inherit all things! My goodness gracious, I could write a whole book on this alone. For the super rich who are reading this book, you do have at least a small idea about inheritance. For the rest of us, let me put it to you this way: The believer is a joint heir with GOD. GOD is your PERFECT FATHER, and you are His son or daughter. All that is GOD's is yours also, a part of your inheritance. GOD Himself is your inheritance! JESUS is your Inheritance! Since Jesus is going to create a new Heaven and a new earth, the new Heaven and new earth will be yours! That's why Jesus told the rich man, "If thou will be perfect, go and sell all that you have, and give to the poor, and you will have treasure in Heaven; and come and follow me." For you rich people, calm down; you don't have to sell all that you own. That was the word of the Lord for that particular rich man, because He knew that man's heart. Jesus was trying to help him see the error of his ways. If you're rich now, go help someone who is in need. If you think you have something now, just wait until you get home to Heaven. All the more you will have. Every son or daughter of GOD who is here on earth now is richer than anyone here on earth who is without the LORD. We are joint heirs with CHRIST! Wow! Our inheritance far surpasses what we have now. Remember a hundredfold? I am sure it is more than that! But to be honest, who cares—as long as I am with God!

Shall I continue on? I think I will. An angel carried John to a great and high mountain and showed that great city, the holy Jerusalem, descending out of Heaven from God. Obviously, there are mountains and hills in Heaven. That is why the angel had to take John to a great, high mountain to see it. As you will soon see, the angel measures the city. Also, GOD Himself lights the city with His own glory, sort of like our sun today. For instance, today in New York, it is cloudy and raining. I can't see the sun, but I know it is daytime because the glory of its light lights the day. GOD is far BRIGHTER than the sun, and His glory lights all of Heaven.

> Having the glory of God and her light was like unto a stone most precious, even like a jasper stone, clear as crystal; And had a wall great and high, and had twelve gates, and at the gates twelve angels, and the names written thereon, which are the

names of the twelve tribes of the children of Israel. The New Jerusalem is a perfect cube from top to bottom. On the east three gates; on the north three gates; on the south three gates; and on the west three gates. The walls of the city have twelve foundations. On the foundations are the names of the twelve apostles of Jesus. (Rev. 21:11–14)

The angel who talked with John had with him a ruler made of pure gold so that the angel could measure the city. Obviously, tools in Heaven would be made of gold. It's not like GOD needs a gold Snap-on truck. The golden ruler is for our benefit, so that we would know that what we are about read are real measurements of a real city. Again, Heaven is a real place.

The city is laid out like a square, as long as it is wide. The angel measured the city with ruler and found it to be 1,400 miles or about 2,200 kilometers in length, and as wide and as high as it is long. The walls of the city are 216 feet thick by man's measurement, which the angel was using. The walls are made of Jasper, and city of pure gold, as pure as glass. (Rev. 21:15–18)

Think of our city Jerusalem here on earth. The great walls around the new city would be 216 feet thick and made of the best jasper ever. Now, think of the twelve gates made of one giant pearl each. Each gate made of one huge pearl! With the city being 1,400 miles tall and the walls 216 feet thick and with each gate made of one single pearl, they'd have to be twelve of the largest pearls ever. Now imagine everything on the inside of the walls of Jerusalem made of the purest gold! Wow! The homes and the ground—everything made of the purest gold. I imagine that the gold there is so shiny and so pure that it looks like you're looking through glass. In the New Jerusalem:

The foundations of the city walls are decorated with every kind of precious stone. The first foundation was jasper, the second sapphire, the third chalcedony, the fourth emerald, the

51

fifth sardonyx, the sixth carnelian, the seventh chrysotile, the eighth beryl, the ninth topaz, the tenth chrysoprase, the eleventh jacinth, and the twelfth amethyst. The twelve gates were twelve pearls, and each gate made of a single pearl. The great street of the city is of pure gold, like transparent glass. (Rev. 22:19–21)

There is no temple in the New Jerusalem, "because the Lord God Almighty and the Lamb are its temple. The city does not need the sun or the moon to shine on it, for the glory of God gives it light, and the Lamb is its lamp" (Rev. 21:22–23).

When the city is here on the new earth:

The nations will walk by its light, and the kings of the earth will bring their splendor into it. On no day will its gates ever be shut, for there is no night there. The glory and honor of the nations will be brought into it. The book of life is in the city, and only those whose names are written in the Lamb's book of life can go in. (Rev. 22:24–27)

In the middle of the city is the river of life. Look at Revelation 22:1: "Then the angel showed me the river of the water of life, as clear as crystal, flowing from the throne of God and of the Lamb." There are not two thrones; it is the throne of God and of the Lamb. Jesus is the Lamb that sits on the throne as God. Keeping it simple, the truth is that God became a man, Jesus, and HE did it to SAVE us.

The river of life runs down the middle of the great city. On each side of the river stood the tree of life, bearing twelve crops of fruit, yielding its fruit every month. And the leaves of the tree are for the healing of the nations. No longer will there be any curse. The throne of God and of the Lamb is in the city, and His servants will serve Him. They will see His face, and His name will be on their foreheads. (Rev. 22:2–4)

For those you that love tattoos, sorry—in Heaven, there is only one, the one that matters most—HIS NAME. Yes, the name of our SAVIOR will be right on our foreheads.

> There will be no more night. They will not need the lamp or the light of the sun, for the Lord God will give them light. And they will reign forever and ever. The angel said to me, "These words are trustworthy and true. The Lord, the God of the spirits of the prophets, sent His angel to show His servants the things that must soon take place."
> "Behold, I am coming soon! Blessed is he who keeps the word of the prophecy in this book."
> I, John, am the one who heard and saw these things. And when I had heard and seen them, I fell down to worship at the feet of the angel who was showing them to me. But he said to me, "Do not do it! I am a fellow servant with you and with your brothers the prophets and of all who keep the words of this book. Worship God!" (Rev. 22:5–9)

As you just read, Heaven is a very real place indeed, with a city with people and angels going in and out. Again, as I mentioned in the earlier chapters, our loved ones are alive! It's awesome! Notice that the angel said to John that he is a fellow servant with his brothers the prophets. That's why GOD, when He appeared to Moses in the burning bush, said, "I am the GOD of Abraham, Isaac, and Jacob." GOD is the GOD of the living and not the dead.

This almost brings to a close this chapter, "Heaven Is a Real Place." For those of you who may be still struggling with the fear of death, let the LORD JESUS have the final word on life after death. As it is today, so it was in Jesus's time: there were people there who didn't believe there was life after death. Those religious teachers were called the Sadducees. Turn to Matthew 22:23, and let's see what our Lord's answer to the life-after-death question was. And, as always, here are the scriptures, starting from Matthew 22:23 and ending at verse 33:

That same day, the Sadducees, who say there is no resurrection, came to Him with a question. "Teacher," they said, "Moses told us that if a man dies without having children, his brother must marry the widow and have children for him. Now there were seven brothers among us. The first one married and died, and since he had no children, he left his wife to his brother. The same thing happened to the second and third brother, right on down to the seventh. Finally, the woman died. Now then, at the resurrection, whose wife will she be of the seven, since all of them were married to her?" Jesus replied, "You are in error, because you do not know the scriptures or the power of God. At the resurrection, people will neither marry nor be given in marriage; they will be like angels in Heaven. But about the resurrection of the dead—have you not read what God said to you, 'I am the God of Abraham, the God of Isaac, and the God of Jacob'? He is not the God of the dead but of the living." When the crowds heard this, they were astonished at His teaching.

Some of you reading this book today are astonished at its teaching. Here you have the LORD JESUS putting the finishing touches on this chapter, "Heaven Is a Real Place." For those of you who were taught that your loved ones are sleeping in the grave, that is not true. He is not the God of the dead but of the Living. "To be absent in the body is to be present with the Lord." They told you this because they didn't know the scripture or the power of God. In Heaven, there is no marriage. We are all just sisters and brothers with one Father God. And for those of you who still believe that while dead, people are sleeping in the grave, waiting for the resurrection, here is JESUS's answer: "Have you not read what God said to you, 'I am the God of Abraham, the God of Isaac, and the God of Jacob'? He is not the God of the dead but of the Living."

As I begin to close this chapter, "Heaven Is a Real Place," I challenge you read, study, and pray for yourself to get more understanding and wisdom from GOD. There is more in the Bible that explains about Heaven than this or any book can ever explain. We are able to grow spiritually in GOD as He reveals more of Himself to us. I am sure that after this book is published, I also will have learned more. Yes, that's the way it is with JESUS our LORD: the closer you get to Him, the more you learn of Him. I pray that your heart is filled with joy as you were reminded that your family is not lost or gone forever but instead are with the LORD. They are doing way better than us, that's for sure!

For some of you who are really sick and are almost going home to Heaven, I pray that everything I have shared will help in taking the fear out of death. I pray that you will look forward to leaving this body and getting your new one that will last forever! Pray for one another, ask GOD to heal you, but know that if you have put your trust in the Lord Jesus Christ, to be with HIM is always far better. Your last breath here is your next breath in Heaven alive, not sleeping in the grave. For those of you who have gone to funerals and heard the preacher say that "they are resting and in a better place," now you know that they really are in a better place for sure.

Give it some thought. Meditate on seeing the LORD JESUS CHRIST face to face. Think about everyone else you will see there also and about the beautiful city there, the New Jerusalem. HEAVEN is a place so filled with GOD's love and GOD's peace, where people are forever happy with no worries or the cares of this life. GOD desires that you think of heavenly things. Colossians 3:2 "Think on things that are from above." GOD is alive, and JESUS, and everyone there is LIVING. Also, for those of you who love animals, when JESUS creates the brand new earth, there will be animals:

> Righteousness will be his belt and faithfulness the sash around his waist, the wolf will live with the lamb, the leopard will lie down with the goat, the calf and the lion and the yearling together; and a little child will lead them. The cow will feed with the bear, their young will lie down together, and the lion will eat straw like an ox. The infant will play near the hole of the cobra, and the young child put his hand into the viper's nest. They will neither harm nor destroy on my entire holy mountain, for the earth will be full of the knowledge of the Lord as

the waters cover the sea. In that day, the root of Jesse will stand
as a banner for the people; the nations will rally to Him, and
His place of rest will be glorious." (Isa.11:5–10)

So you see, all in Heaven are Living in love, peace, and harmony with one
another and GOD. JESUS is going to remake everything that you see today by
starting from scratch. He will make a new earth, stars, galaxies, universe—
everything. The new earth will be filled with all the animals and beauty, as it
was before sin entered the world and wrecked this one. Go back on your own
and read Genesis 1 and 2. Everything that transpired in Genesis 1 and 2 will
be again. There you will see exactly how God wanted it to be in the beginning. Remember that CHRIST said, "Behold, I make all things new." Yes, ALL
THINGS will be NEW. Then GOD will send down the New Jerusalem, and
the LORD and His people will live together in peace and harmony forever. But
for now, all of our loved ones that BELIEVED are in Heaven—alive and waiting for that day. Heaven is the land of the living. HEAVEN is a REAL PLACE.

CHAPTER 6

Call of the Names

This is the simplest chapter in this book but also the MOST IMPORTANT chapter. GOD IS CALLING you—and every person still holding back—by name. GOD is calling the following names. Some names are written more than once. Some God has called more than once to LIFE with Him forever. GOD wants to write the following names in the LAMB'S BOOK of LIFE. CHRIST JESUS is the LAMB of GOD. Some of the names written below are in the book of life already. JESUS made this possible with His own blood. Here are words of Jesus in red representing His blood poured out for the following names. "Behold I stand at the door and knock; if any man hears My voice and opens the door, I will come in to him, and I will sup with him, and he with Me. Verily, verily, I say unto you, he that heareth My word and believeth on Him that sent Me has everlasting life and shall not come into condemnation but is passed from death unto life."

God is calling you! Jesus is calling you! Here is the call of the names:

Mike, Tommy, Hao, Shirley, Toney, Eddie, Ann, Anna, Jimmy, Bobby, Joe, Stella, Karen, Hal, Naomi, Janice, Robert, Richard, Crystal, Carmelo, Jamel, John, Sharon, Michelle, Tapio, Lin-Lin, Justin, Justice, Neyra, Edward, Jason, Tracy, Mel, Gregg, Nat, Vincent, Marques, Elias, Jeremy, Elijah, Daniel, Samantha, Rosemarie, Lien, Albert, Maria, Gale, Steve, Isabel, William, Christine, Carl, Dave, David, Scott, Louis, Beth, Janette, Janet, Walker, Walt, Amare, Shelia, François, Glen, Curtis, Dan, Kenny, Roger, Tammy, Margret, Renishaw, Cheyenne, Jace, Doug, Jennifer, Regina, Rihanna, Rhianna, James, Kellie, Jessica, Matthew, Ariel, Ethan, Angela, Camille, Jutta, Elaine, Enza, Enzi, Corrine, Noel, Tom, Larry, Jackie, Kyle, Susan, Kate, Kim, Anthony, Jillian, Kevin, Tasanee, Laura, Melanie, Mary,

Alexia, Alexis, Alexa, Allison, Courtney, Rachel, Hajime, Melissa, Ivy, Heidi, Barbara, Keolani, Aliyah, Esther, Cliff, Liz, Elizabeth, Fantasia, Huang, Gina, Phyllis, Claudia, Karen, Andrew, Ryan, Zach, Zack, Zackary, Zachariah, Jeremiah, Dwayne, Enoye, Khaliah, Andrea, Thomas, John, Danny, Jake, Michael, Carlos, Howie, Aaron, Nicole, Elaine, Sean, Patrick, Devante, Loreini, Lawrence, Daniel, Gary, Deidra, Ishan, Stephano, Stephanie, Jamel, Yori, Coby, Chelsea, Christopher, Donna, Lenny, Quinn, Liam, Marissa, Sondra, Sandra, Genesis, Raven, Steven, Kristen, Stephen, Hilda, Edith, Jose, Joshua, Evlise, Wesley, Jeziel, Corey, Teresa, Frank, Toni, Kurt, Johnny, Kris, Antonio, Vincenzo, Daniel, Caleb, Justin, Sara, Rebekah, Rebecca, Katie, Chun, Katherine, Tatsuo, Kathy, Nikki, Vinny, Matt, Douglas, Jen, Debbie, Jimmy, Judy, Paul, Chastity, Rich, Richard, Ashley, Shay, Lucy, Torian, Lindsey, Myllasa, Aria, Jess, Ali, Keith, Copper, Colin, CJ, Marilyn, Stacey Ann, Stacey, Lauren, Ellen, Gabriella, Gabby, Arianna, Rashida, Irini, Joseph, Joey, Krystal, Lei, Jian, Desiree, Yoon, Mikael, Rainer, Cindy, Lillian, Lillana, Elena, Seth, Sam, Sammy, Jamie, Zhuang, Kyra, Danielle, Mark, Garrett, Kana, Kayla, Katelynn, Akahana, Catelynn, Zacharia, Katherine, Vito, Mark, Kim, George, Aggie, Bill, Willie, Victor, Dean, Patrick, Jennifer, Val, Janet, Lois, Ezekiel, Marlon, Pat, Angelo, Ronda, Rainer, Tyson, Raymond, Cong, Marcus, Allen, Eli, Jr. Lin, Even, Pierre, Don, Kevin, Ester, Apollonia, Ralph, Darrel, Carol, Ron, Danny, Fumi, Ganahara, Heather, Frances, Fay, Abhiti, Vanisha, Tara, Paul, Vicky, Donald, Dee Girl, Hector, Nelson, Frank, Lynette, I Anna, Rakia, Zakia, Silvia, Barack, Hue, Mary, Martha, Priscilla, Kent, Sylvester, Aito, Donna, Horace, Peter, Rudy, Albert, Maria, Charles, Neil, Andre, Arvin, Audrey, Aurea, Colin, Dhina, Elizabeth, Errol, Jun, Gerry, Jack, Joanne, Rosario, Dexter, Ethan, Ariel, Josie, Derek, Meagan, Hibiki, Trisha, Gangol, Amanda, Kelly, Kirk, Sally, Kate, Shaquille, Doug, Ed, Tina, Tiny, Isaiah, Rachel, Adam, Troy, Abdul, Dean, Matthew, Timothy, Brittney, Jazelle, Gladys, Donnie, Boomer, Karin, Kimi, Gunnar, Boa, Carlton, Jiao, Rosie, Shelly, Rosaria, Johan, Monique, Jose, Ezra, Joel, Sal, Mona, Meital, Molly, Richie, Bam, Joji, Teba, Reba, Maureen, Katie, Tom, Tony, Juan, Jay, Bik, Jesus, Carmen, Carman, Lisa, Liza, Solomon, Haggai, Ruth, Gideon,

Jeremiah, Hy, Omri, Eva, Lizzie, Petey, Elvis, Sidney, Alex, Winston, Faith, Winter, Summer, Prince, Princess, Ray, Raymond, Lamont, Aadi, Aamina, Chiemi, Chieye, Zi, Zhuo, Takara, Tamayo, Gao, Hatsu, Hideaki, Harue, Hang, Isako, Jaya, Jorani, Jin, Kanya, Kana, An, Jess, Jeff, Cece, Sandy, Sophia, Emma, Isabella, Olivia, Lily, Chloe, Madison, Emily, Abigail, Addison, Madelyn, Ella, Hailey, Kaylee, Avery, Brooklyn, Peyton, Layla, Hannah, Alden, Alton, Jackson, Mason, Liam, Jacob, Jayden, Noah, Lucas, Logan, Caden, Connor, Brayden, Benjamin, Nicholas, Alexander, Daren, Alexandra, Landon, Charlotte, Natalie, Grace, Amelia, Arianna, Gabriella, Elsie, Lillian, Makayla, Alyssa, Yi, Yun, Isabelle, Savannah, Evelyn, Leah, Keria, Lucy, Taylor, Lauren, Harper, Scarlet, Brianna, Piao Mai, Mei, Victoria, Liliana, Aria, Annabelle, Gianna, Kennedy, Julia, Bailey, Jordyn, Nora, Caroline, Mackenzie, Jasmine, Jocelyn, Kendall, Ricardo, Morgan, Nevaeh, Brooke, Aniweta, Penelope, Violet, Hadley, Ashlyn, Sadie, Paige, Qiao, Sienna, Piper, Nathan, Dylan, Andrew, Gabriel, Gavin, Owen, Carter, Tyler, Christian, Wyatt, Tisha, Henry, Joseph, Max, Grayson, Christopher, Concetta, Contessa, Levi, Charlie, Dominic, Oliver, Chase, Cooper, Tristan, Colton, Austin, Hunter, Saveria, Parker, Ian, Jordan, Cole, Julian, Asad, Carson, Miles, Blake, Brody, Sebastian, Adrian, Nolan, Fortunato, Francesca, Fortunato, Giacomo, Gracja, Grazia, Sean, Zeta, Riley, Bentley, Xavier, Asher, Dino, Micah, Josiah, Nathaniel, Bryson, Ryder, Bryce, Kourtney, Rosa, Arnett, Terry, Venetia, Nance, Patricia, Emily, Lucy, Giada, Vonetta, Ankoma, Loverme, Robyn, Kirby, Gloria, Yvetteliz, Murphy, Dale, Dottie, Mary Lou, Jules, Mary, Leann, Dotty, Laverne, Linda, Brenda, Viridiana, Tyrone, Sultana, Pamela, Mario, Puffy, Danica, Shaun, Dwight, Justin, George, Mildred, Vinnie, Irene, Abam, Abassi, Addolorata, Carisa, Carlo, Elisio, Bruce, Cliff, Guido, Rufino, Stephanos, Virgilio, Zola, Carlos, Sandy, Sandra, Vanessa, Valdis, Vanity, Lee, David, Tory, Pierre, Ed, Edward, Josephine, Josie, Josellys, Derrick, Emilio, Ariel, Gabriel, Reina, Luis, Dominique, Angel, Marques, Michelle, Guillermo, Peter, Jim, Maricela, Marymadeline, Jeremiah, Jedidiah, Rose, Sharon, Luke, Khaleesi, Jaechelle, Armani, Ackmed, Lee, Laura, Adam, Eve, Steven, Paul, Rebecca, Anthony, Michael, Bruce, Devin, Blake, Ronald,

Donald, Jake, Jace, Justin, Barbara, Dora, Doris, Liam, Nancy, Maria, Dolores, Lourdes, Eric, Tuty, Katie, Mark, Marcus, Trina, Tina, Jose, Joel, Frank, Soel, Nida, Leonida, Lonnard, Lonnie, Junior, Heather, Cathy, Casey, Bob, Beatriz, Sara, Sarai, William, Winston, Wilma, Denise, Destiny, Justice, Miracle, Leslie, Curt, Cain, Abel, Joy, Joyce, Martha, Lauren, Carl, Danny, Daniel, _____ _____ _____ _____ _____ _____

_____ _____ _____ _____ _____ _____

_____ _____ _____ _____ _____ _____

_____ _____ _____ _____ _____

_____ _____ _____ _____ _____

_____ _____ _____ _____ _____

_____ _____ _____ _____ _____

_____ _____ _____ _____ _____

_____ _____ _____ _____ _____

_____ _____ _____ _____ _____

_____ _____ _____ _____ _____

_____ _____ _____ _____ _____

_____ _____ _____ _____ _____

_____ _____ _____ _____ _____

_____ _____ _____ _____

_____ _____ _____ _____

_____ _____ _____ _____

_____ _____ _____ _____

_____ _____ _____ _____

_____ _____ _____ _____

_____ _____

If you did not see your name and you want God's great love and forgiveness, here is your chance. GOD is giving you a very unique opportunity. You get to write your name into the book of life. By signing your name, you are asking Jesus to forgive you for all of your sins—your sins from the past, your sins now, and your sins in the future. By signing, you are confiming that you want Jesus's love and the Father's Holy Spirit living in you. Your signature confirms that you want Jesus to be both your Lord and Savior. Those spaces are for you, your family, and your friends. If they want God's unfailing love and mercy, all they have to do sign, and they will receive His Holy Spirit. God has promised that before you even finish your signature, you will already be written into the book of life, which is in Heaven. Heaven is a real place.

CHAPTER 7

Seven Questions from Tommy

ere are some questions some people have for God but are afraid to ask:

Question #1:   If there is a Heaven, why is there an earth? Why have the middleman?

Question #2:   If you play telephone with six people, and the original story changes among just these six, then how can you believe the Bible, which was written so many years ago?

Question #3:   If there is truly a GOD, then why would He allow a devil to do evil?

Question #4:   There were many myths written when man could not understand the answers to things. Could the Bible's Adam and Eve story be a myth?

Question #5:   If the Bible is truly the book of all books, then why are there so many forms of the Bible and so many different beliefs and religions?

Question #6:   If Jesus Christ came to earth as the Lord's son, then why does He not send Him back in this time realm to make people believe?

Question #7:   I always save the best for last. Many years ago, when people did not have any kind of scientific evidence to answer the questions they had, they created myths about them to provide comfort. Now, with this being known, when people died in front of other people, there must have been much chaos—people crying and wondering why their loved ones were gone. They did not understand that life comes to an end or why. So, here's the question: How do we know a wise old Jewish man did not just decide to write the whole Bible to comfort all of these people just so that they would not be afraid of dying?

The preceding questions are from a friend of mine named Tommy. He and his wonderful wife, Janet, gave me the honor and privilege to speak at their wedding. These are questions he had and wanted answers for. He felt that many people have the same questions but are afraid to ask them. People are afraid to ask question about GOD and His people. Maybe all of your life you have been told, "You don't question GOD!" Well, that is not true. GOD welcomes your questions. He loves you—why wouldn't He want you to ask Him questions? Those who told you not to question GOD really don't understand the scriptures or the love of GOD. Can you imagine telling someone, "I really, truly love you and would die for you, but you cannot ask me any questions"? Come on, now—really! For some people, it may be that they are afraid to hear the answers, so they'd rather not ask Him, or maybe they fear that He won't answer at all. These are the "you don't question God!" people. Well, I know for sure that GOD answers prayers and questions. Sometimes He answers right away and sometimes years later—because at some moments in our lives, we may not be ready to understand certain things just yet. There are also certain things that will only be answered when we get to Heaven. But be encouraged, because there is a lot that GOD will reveal to you while here on Earth.

OK, since Tommy asked these questions of me, I will try my best to answer them the best I can. I am also going to add some more questions that people have asked me over the years. I will pray and ask for the LORD's help to answer these questions. I challenge you to ask GOD yourself. God will answer you. This way, to use Tommy's words, you can cut out the "middleman."

Question #8: If GOD loves people, why is He sending some of them to hell?

Question #9: If GOD is good, why do little children and good people get sick, suffer, and die?

Question #10: Why would a kind and good GOD create hell?

Question #11: What about those who have died but never heard about JESUS? Are they in hell?

Question #12: Is it true that when you die, you sleep or rest in the grave until Judgment Day? (Now, this question was answered in the chapters above, but I will share more.)

The Answers

Question #1: If there is a Heaven, why is there an earth? Why have the "middleman"?

Yes, there is a Heaven. That's what this book is about. Heaven is a real place. By the way, Tommy actually asked these questions before I ever wrote a word of this book. I am sure that if Tommy could have read this book first, he wouldn't have asked the questions. But since he did ask this years ago, I will answer it anyway. GOD created the HEAVENS and the earth as an expression of His LOVE. He did it because He loves us and wanted us to have the best. As it was in the beginning, God wanted to live with mankind forever on earth. Before Adam and Eve disobeyed God by eating from the tree of the knowledge of good and evil, they loved God and enjoyed fellowship with Him here on Earth. (For my young readers, Adam and Eve used to "hang out with God on this earth." How cool is that, hanging out with GOD!) Today, we at all ages have the same privilege through His HOLY SPIRIT. We get to "hang out with the Father each day, through His Holy Spirit. But there is nothing like seeing Jesus face to face!

Any loving human parents would want to give their child the best. Well, GOD has given us HIS BEST. HE gave the best to Adam and Eve, even from the beginning. (By the way, whenever you see words written all in CAPITAL letters, especially GOD, JESUS, the HOLY SPIRIT, or HEAVEN, it is a shout out with joy for what God has done!)

Many times a guy uses this line to pick up a girl: "Baby, I will give you the world." Well, only with GOD is this true. This universe, the planets, the stars, the sun, and the moon were all created for all of us. HE really has given us the world! Before, the earth was our home to live with GOD, but now, because of sin, we will have to wait until we get to Heaven to FULLY enjoy our time with HIM. By His HOLY SPIRIT, we can still have great fellowship with HIM here on earth, but in Heaven, there will really be no limits.

In the beginning, GOD gave us everything but one tree!

> "Then the Lord God took the man and put him in the Garden of Eden to tend and keep it. And the Lord God commanded the man, saying "Of every tree of the garden you may freely eat; But of tree of the knowledge of good and evil you shall not eat, for in the day that you eat of it, you shall surely die." (Gen. 2:15–17)

In fact, after man sinned, they hid from God. The Lord had to call him out, because they were hiding.

> And they heard the sound of the Lord God walking in the garden in the cool of the day, and Adam and his wife hid themselves from the presence of the Lord God among the trees of the garden. Then the Lord God called out to Adam and said to him, "Adam, where are you?" So he said, "I heard Your voice in the garden, and I was afraid because I was naked, and I hid myself." (Gen. 3:8–10)

As you can see, God and man lived here in perfect harmony before the fall. The earth is not the middleman—it was supposed to be our home with God forever. But we messed things up. The great news, as we have studied earlier, is that God will destroy this world and make all things new. Then we will live with God forever, like He wanted in the first place.

Before I move on to the next question, I want to take my sister Eve off the hook. Adam was standing right next to Eve and watched the devil trick his wife. If Adam would have stopped the serpent or pulled Eve away, the fall would have never happened. In fact, their eyes weren't open to sin until Adam ate the fruit. Once Adam ate of the fruit, then their eyes were opened, and they knew they were naked.

And the fruit they ate was not an apple. Nowhere in the Bible does it say that the fruit was an apple. The Bible says it was a tree with fruit. And the apples said, "Amen!" The Bible doesn't say what type of fruit, so please, people—you can eat apples again. Let's look at Genesis 3:6: "So when the woman saw that the tree was good for food, that it was pleasant to the eyes, and desirable to make one wise, she took of its fruit and ate. She also gave some to her HUSBAND WITH HER, and HE DID EAT." I put the word *with* in all caps to make the point that Adam was standing right there with her. Cross-check it in your Bible—he was with her. It was as if once she didn't die, he said to himself, "Hmm, it must be OK. Now I will eat," and HE DID EAT. Here is verse 7: "Then the eyes of both of them were opened, and they knew that they were naked; and they sewed fig leaves together and made themselves coverings." Notice that after Adam eats, THEN their eyes were opened. That's why God wasn't having it. They both sinned; they both were at fault. But if the man had done his job and protected the woman, the fall of man never would have happened. That's why the first person God called was Adam: "Where are you?"

Question #2: If you play telephone with six people, and the original changes among just these six, then how can you believe the Bible, which was written so many years ago?

The Bible is the word of GOD, and His word is the same yesterday, today, and forever. The Bible has not changed—it is the same book that it was from the beginning. The Bible is a divine book inspired by GOD and written by men. The Bible is a historic book backed up by world history. Caesar, Herod, and Rome are all in the Bible. It is an infallible record of real, live events with real people. From Genesis to Revelation, the Bible contains sixty-six books. GOD used forty people to write the books. The writers ranged from kings (like David) to fishermen (like Peter). The time span from the first book written by Moses, which is Genesis, to the last book written by John (Revelation) is over four thousand years. The different writers in the Bible—Paul, Moses, John, Joshua, Ruth, to name a few—lived over fifteen hundred years apart. Yet if you read the Bible from Genesis to Revelation, it reads like one large book.

The Bible has predicted 668 prophecies about world events, and every one of them has been fulfilled. The Bible also predicts future world events that will soon come to pass, some of which I will cover in the chapter "The Last Day." No other book can claim that. Why? The Bible is not just a book—it is the word of God written through men. For the word of God is quick and powerful, sharper than any two-edged sword, piercing even to the dividing asunder of soul and spirit, and to the joints and marrow, and is a discerner of thoughts and the intents of the heart. What God says in the Bible always happens. Archeology, the Dead Sea Scrolls, and so on all support and confirm the Bible. The fact is—and it is a fact—that when archeologists dig at a biblical site, they take out the Bible so that they can know what they are looking at.

The Bible covers over four thousand years of men's lives and thousands of stories from different countries, yet it reads like one story. In fact, you can buy the Bible in book form without the verses marked and read it like a book. Isaiah 40: "The grass withers, the flowers fade, but the word of our God shall stand forever." This is true to this very day. The Bible is the most copied and reprinted book in world history. The Bible is the bestselling book in the world—period. The Bible has survived through wars, famines, and the Great Depression. Why? Because it is the word of God.

So, the telephone question helps prove my point. There is no way that man could have done this. If man wrote the Bible, it would always be changing, just like in the telephone game. But the Bible, covering over four thousand years from Genesis to Revelation, is the same—yesterday, today, and forever—unlike the telephone game, where the story changes from person to person. All these different people, all these different places over sixty-six books and forty authors—yet it reads like one person wrote it. That person is God, using men to write down His words. The Bible is printed in every language and in different styles, but all have the same words that God said from the beginning in Genesis: "In the beginning, God created the heavens and the earth." And they are the same words that He said in the end in Revelation: "The grace of our Lord Jesus Christ be with you all. Amen."

Question #3:   If there is truly a GOD, then why would he allow a devil to do evil?

The devil is a fallen angel. The devil was created to worship God. He was leader of the angels who worship God. God even built instruments into his body. God even gave him a great name, Lucifer, which means light bearer. One day, Lucifer got full of himself with pride and decided he didn't want to just worship God—he wanted to exalt himself above God. So, Jesus kicked him and the other fallen angels out of Heaven and threw them down to earth. The great news is that Jesus will cast the devil and his demons/fallen angels into the lake of fire, where they will burn forever. Here is Isaiah 14:12–17:

> How art thou fallen from Heaven, O Lucifer, son of the morning! How art thou cut down to the ground, which didst weaken the nations! For thou hast said in your heart, "I will ascend into Heaven, I will exalt my throne above the stars of God: I will sit also upon the mount of the congregation in the sides of the north: I will ascend above the heights of the clouds; I will be like the Most High." Yet thou shall be brought down to hell, to the sides of the pit.

In Ezekiel 28:13–17, we get a picture of how beautiful the devil was and why he was kicked out of the mountain of God:

> Thou hast been in Eden, the garden of God: every precious stone was thy covering, the Sardis, topaz, and the diamond, the beryl, the onyx, and the jasper, the sapphire, the emerald, and the carbuncle, and the gold: the workmanship of thy taberts and of thy pipes was prepared in thee in the day that thou were created. Thou art the anointed cherub that covered; and I have set thee so: thou were upon the holy mountain of God; thou hast walked up and down in the midst of the stones of fire. Thou were perfect in thy ways from the day that thou were created, until iniquity was found in thee. By the multitude of thy merchandise, they have filled the midst of thee with violence, and thou hast sinned: therefore, I will cast thee as a profane out of the mountain of God, and I will destroy thee, O covering cherub; from the midst of the stones of fire, your heart was lifted up because of thy beauty; thou hast corrupted thy wisdom by the reason of your brightness: I will cast you to the ground; I will lay thee before the kings, that they may behold thee. Thou hast defiled thy sanctuaries by the multitude of your iniquities, by the iniquity of thy traffic; therefore will I bring forth a fire from the midst of thee; it shall devour thee, and I will bring thee to ashes upon the earth in the sight of all that behold thee. All they that know thee among the people shall be astonished at thee; thou shall be a terror, and never shall thou be any more.

So, you see, the devil was a very beautiful angel whom God created. God made him His leader of worship. But he let his beauty and brightness get to him. Instead of always being humble and grateful to Jesus for creating him this way, he let his heart be filled with pride because of his beauty and greatness. Then the devil turned on God, so God will destroy him.

Question #4:   There were many myths written when man could not understand the answers to things. Could the Bible's Adam and Eve story possibly be myth?

First, I will let God answer this question, and then I will make a comment or two. Not that God needs me to say anything. Tommy did ask me the question, and I promised that I would answer. Here is what God said:

> And God said, "Let us make man in Our own image, after Our own likeness, and let them have dominion over the fish of the sea, and over the fowl of the air, and over all the earth, and over every creeping thing that creepeth upon the earth." So God created man in His own image, in the image of God created He him: male and female created He them. And God blessed them, and said unto them, "Be fruitful, and multiply, and replenish the earth, and subdue it; and have dominion over the fish of the sea and over the fowl of the air, and over every living thing that moves upon the earth." (Gen. 1:26–28)

Here is how God did it:

> And the Lord God formed man of the dust of the ground, and breathed into his nostrils the breath of life; and man became a living soul. (Gen. 2:7)
>
> And the Lord God caused a deep sleep to fall upon Adam, and he slept: and He took one of his ribs, and closed up the flesh instead thereof; And from the rib, which the Lord God had taken from the man, made He a woman, and brought her unto the man. And Adam said, "This is now bone of my bones, and flesh of my flesh; she shall be called woman because she was taken out of man. Therefore shall a man leave his father and

mother and shall cleave unto his wife, and they shall be one flesh." (Gen. 2:21–24)

OK—now, my turn. To be honest, what is there left to say? God said it all. But here is my answer. Number one, God said it. Number two, God said it. Number three, God said it. Number four, Adam and Eve were the first two humans ever created and are historical facts. You can look this up in any reference books, like the dictionary, encyclopedias, and so on. People, Adam and Eve were the father and mother of us all. Every human being came from Adam and Eve's being fruitful and multiplying. People, think about it—what God said is the only thing that makes sense. We are living proof. The only way you or I got into this world was through our moms and dads. Male sperm fertilizes a female egg, and then nine months later, Mom has a baby. If you could follow the family tree of every human being all the way back, it leads to Adam and Eve.

Because he didn't want to believe God, man has come up with all kinds of theories that don't make any sense. We come from apes? This is the dumbest of all. Apes can only reproduce apes. We spend millions of dollars each year looking for the missing link when a ten-dollar Bible has the answer. Every animal that God created only reproduces the same type of animal. That's how God created them, and that is the way it has been from the day God did it. An ape can't even have a baby chimp, so how are we to believe that man came from apes? Come on, now—think about it. What about the apes in the zoo? Did they decide "Nah, we are cool. We will just stay apes"? Who needs to date supermodels and drive your own car? Human beings are not animals. Humans are men and women and children created in the image of God. In the image of God created He him. Male and female created He them. A pregnant goat has a baby goat. A cow has a baby calf. A horse has a baby horse. A man makes love to his wife, and nine months later, she has a baby human, just like God intended. So to answer your question, Tommy, Adam and Eve were real people and the father and mother of us all. By the way, which came first—the chicken or the egg? The chicken came first, just as God created it. The rooster and hen made love, and the hen laid the egg. The egg hatched a baby chick, maybe in the sun. And that chick was another chicken, not a hot girl!

Question #5:   If the Bible is truly the book of all books, then
                 why are there so many forms of the Bible and
                 so many different beliefs and religions?

Again, Tommy, you helped me answer the question. The reason there are so many forms of the Bible is because the Bible is, to quote you, "the book of books." The Bible is the only true and real word of God. The true believer wants and studies the Bible, which is the holy word of God. Think of it as God's love letters to you. There all kinds of people in the world today—Indian, Chinese, French, German, Spanish, Irish, to name just a few. Now, think of all the different kinds of people in this world. As you can see, men and women of God come in all shapes and colors. Some speak English; some don't. Each of these nations needs their own word of God in their own language. Then there are different styles of Bibles. The King James, the Living Translation, the New International, the New King James (not LeBron James), to name a few. There are different types of Bibles—Life Application Bible, New Believer's Bible, Concordance Bible, Spanish to English, English to Russian, Greek to Arab, to name a few. Then there are electronic Bibles, online Bibles, DVDs, flash-drive Bibles—I could go on and on. But you get the point—there are many different people with different needs, and that's why there are so many different Bibles.

As far as religions and beliefs, people make the same mistake today that Adam and Eve did. They don't want to obey God, so they make it up as they go. They don't want to obey the holy book, the Bible, so they make up their own stuff. Even worse, some know that the Bible is the only word of God, but they obey only part of the Bible. Jesus came and gave His life for the sins of the world. He is the way, the truth, and the life. He wants to be and deserves to be Lord of your life. He gave His life for you, as you well know if you're this far into this book. But, sadly, people want to have God without Jesus or God on their own terms. Jesus challenges us to live righteously and to love people no matter what:

Blessed are the poor in spirit, for theirs is the kingdom of Heaven.
Blessed are they that mourn, for they shall be comforted. Blessed

are the meek, for they shall inherit the earth. Blessed are they which do hunger and thirst after righteousness, for they shall be filled. Blessed are the merciful, for they shall obtain mercy. Blessed are the pure in heart, for they shall see God. Blessed are the peacemakers, for they shall be called the children of God. Blessed are they which are persecuted for righteousness' sake: for theirs is the kingdom of Heaven. Blessed are ye, when men shall revile you and persecute you, and say all manner of evil against you falsely for my sake. Rejoice, and be exceeding glad, for great is your reward in Heaven, for so persecuted they the prophets which were before you. (Matt 5:3–11)

Some people just don't want to obey the Holy Bible, the holy word of God, so they make up their own book and call it God's holy word. Some say that angels told them this is the new way. Some just wrote a science fiction novel and made their own religion. Some people, like their father the devil, think that they are smarter than the God. They tried to outslick God and mixed Jesus's words into their own rules and regulations. Here is God's answer to the question about different beliefs and religions. I tend to be long in answers; Jesus tends to get right to the heart of the matter. Here is God's answer:

I marvel that you are so soon removed from Him that called you into the grace of Christ unto another gospel: Which is not another; but there be some that trouble you, and would pervert the Gospel of Christ. But though we, or an angel from Heaven, preach any other gospel unto you than that which we have preached unto you, let him be accursed. As we said before, so say I now again: if any man preaches any other gospel unto you than that you have received, let him be accursed.

That answer came from God. He knew man would try to do his own thing before we were created. That answer is in the holy word of God, the Bible, from Galatians 1:6–9. The answer, my friend, is not blowing in the wind—the answer is in the word of God!

> Question #6:   If Jesus Christ came to earth as the Lord's son, then why does He not send Him back in this time realm to make people believe?

First of all, we all know that the Lord and Jesus are the same person. But again, to defend Tommy, he asked these questions years ago, before this book was written, when this book was just a thought. You who have read your Bible or this book up this point know that the Lord is gracious and full of compassion. He is slow to anger and of great mercy. The Lord is good to all, and His tender mercies are over all His work. The Lord is not slack concerning His promise to return, as some men count slackness, but He is long suffering toward us, not willing that any should perish but that all should come to repentance. The Lord Jesus is trying to wait for every single soul to come to his or her senses, repent, and turn to Him. Look at how much He loves—even after the cross, He is still giving man one last chance. He is using everything to try to reach out to mankind before He comes back to destroy this world and those who don't believe.

He wrote the Bible and sent preachers, teachers, prophets, and nuns. If they won't study their Bible, I will try to reach them by a book. If they will not read a book, I will use the Internet. If they don't have computers, I will name people, places, and things here on earth after people, places, and things in my holy word and Heaven—Saint Mark's Place, Saint John's Place, Holy Cross High school, Christ the King High School, Calvary Cemetery. His name shall be John; I will name her Mary. I have two friends who live across the street from me. They are from Africa. Know what their names are? Their names are Mary and Joseph. These aren't Afro-Americans like me. They are Africans who lived in Africa and came to America. Yet they were named after Mother Mary and Joseph from the Bible.

The Lord Jesus is waiting as long as He can for that one last soul. Don't be fooled—today is the day of salvation! You could be the person He is waiting for. The Lord Jesus will not wait forever! But the day of the Lord will come as a thief in the night. The Heavens will disappear with a roar, the elements will be destroyed by fire, and the earth and everything in it will be laid bare. Since everything will be destroyed in this way, what kind of people ought you to be? You ought to live holy and godly lives as you look forward to the day of God and speed its coming. That day will bring about destruction of the heavens by fire, and the elements will melt in the heat. But keeping with His promise, we are looking forward to the new Heaven and new earth, the home of righteousness.

> Question #7:   I always like to save the best for last, so here you go. Many years ago, when people did not have any kind of scientific evidence to answer the questions they had, they created myths to answer these questions and even "comfort" them (this is fact). Now, with this being known, when people died in front of other people, there must have been much chaos—people crying and wondering why their loved ones were gone, not understanding that life comes to an end—just like an old part that needs replacing on a vehicle. How do we know a wise old Jewish man did not decide to begin writing the whole Bible to comfort all these people just so that they would not be afraid of dying?

Well, Tommy, again you have blessed me by helping me with the answer. A wise old Jewish man *did* write the Bible. One of the reasons the old Jewish man wrote the Bible was to take the fear out of death and comfort those left behind. And He is pretty old indeed. The man, Lord forgive me, is older than dirt. He is the great I AM. He was, He is, and He is to come. In the beginning was the Word, and the Word was with God, and the Word was God. He was in the beginning with God. All things were made through Him, and without Him nothing was made that was made. In Him was life, and the life was the light of men. He is the image of the invisible God, the first born over all creation. For by Him all things were created: things in Heaven and on earth, visible and invisible, whether thrones or powers or rulers or authorities. All things were created by Him and for Him. He is before all things, and in Him, all things hold together. For God was pleased to have all of His fullness dwell in Him. The writer of the Bible is both God and Jewish. He is Lord Jesus the Christ.

> Question #8: If GOD loves people, why is He sending some of them to hell?

Hell was not made for us. That's right! Hell was not made for any human being. Hell was made for the devil and his demons. No human should want to go to hell, nor *should* they go to hell. God doesn't send anyone to hell. *We* choose to go. It is our choice. Every day is Father's Day. You can choose God to be your Father, and when your life here on earth is over, you will live with God the Father forever. Or you can choose the devil to be your father, and when you leave this earth, you will suffer with the devil in torment forever. Choose Jesus, who paid for your sins, to be your Father, and live forever. Or you can choose the devil to be your father, pay for your own sins, and burn with the devil forever. If you are still unsure about which father you should choose, please read this book again. But make no mistake—God doesn't send people to hell. They choose to go. Choose Jesus, and live forever. Do nothing, and burn forever. It is your choice.

> Question #9: If GOD is good, why do little children and good people get sick, suffer, and die?

God *is* good, and He never intended for man to get sick and die. When God made this world, He blessed this world. The world was perfect, without sickness or death. Man had the same choice then that he has today. Trust and obey God, and live forever. Man brought sickness and death into this world when he chose to disobey God. The amazing thing is that God warned us this would happen. Genesis 2:16–17 says: "And the Lord God commanded the man, 'You are free to eat from any tree in the garden; but you must not eat from the tree of the knowledge of good and evil, for when you eat of it, you will surely die.'"

Unfortunately, man didn't listen; thus, our sin brought sickness and death into this world. As a result, people get sick, die, and leave this world. But I thank God that Heaven is a real place, because when a child leaves here, he or she goes to Jesus and lives forever. Every one of those little children that were shot in the Sandy Hook school shooting in New Town, Connecticut, went to be with Jesus and are alive right now as you are reading this book. Every one of those teachers that mimicked our Lord Jesus by giving his or her life trying to save the children is in Heaven with God today—alive! That final act of kindness, trying to save His little ones from the acts of the devil, was enough to be accounted to them as righteousness!

> Psalms 116:15: "Precious in the sight of the Lord is the death of His saints."
>
> Isaiah 57:1: "The righteous perish, and no one ponders it in his heart; devout men are taken away, and no one understands that the righteous are taken away to be spared from evil."

And we will see them again!

Question #10: Why would a kind and good GOD create hell?

God did not create hell for people. He created hell to punish the devil and his angels. But some people choose to go to hell. Think about this: if there were no hell, the devil and his people would get away with murder. They could do all the evil they wanted and then kill themselves, and that would be it. But the truth is that an evil person's last breath on earth is his or her next breath in hell, to live in torment forever! Hitler, terrorists, and so on—all, like the rich man, are in hell today in torment, waiting for worse—the LAKE OF FIRE! One of the dumbest things I ever heard a person say was, "I don't care if I go to Heaven or hell. I have friends in both." Well, people, you'd better care, because just as Heaven is a real place, hell is also a real place. But hell was not created for us.

Here are the words of Jesus from Matthew 25:41: "Then shall He say also unto them on the left hand, 'Depart from me, ye cursed, into everlasting fire, prepared for the devil and his angels.'"

> Question #11:   What about those who have died and never
> heard about JESUS? Are they in hell?

God is a loving and just God. Jesus paid the price for the sins of everybody once and for all. If a person dies without knowing about Jesus, God will take this into consideration. But no one who ends up in hell will be able to say that God was unfair. By the time people end up in hell, they have nobody to blame but themselves, and they know it. For the wrath of God is revealed from Heaven against all ungodliness and unrighteousness of men who suppress the truth in unrighteousness, because that which is known of God is revealed in them, for God revealed it to them. For the invisible things of Him from the creation of the world are clearly seen, being understood by the things that are made, even His eternal power and Godhead, so that they are without excuse.

> Question #12:   Is it true that when you die, you sleep or rest
> in the grave until Judgment Day?

No, you don't sleep or rest in your grave. As I stated in some chapters before this, your last breath on earth is your next breath in Heaven alive. One of the main reasons the LORD had me write this book was to dispel this myth. I have gone to many funerals at which the pastor says, "Oh, so-and-so is in a better place," but then he doesn't describe the place. Many people are told that when others die, they are asleep and resting, which is why children and even some adults are afraid to go to bed after a funeral. Yet the LORD ordained this book to be written so that you will now know where they are. Now you know for certain that they are in a far better place than you could ever imagine! You will now be able to describe to your children the "better place." You can say that they are in the New Jerusalem in Heaven alive! You can tell them that JESUS is alive! The people with Him are alive! He is the GOD and LORD of the living! HEAVEN for sure is a REAL PLACE!

> "To be absent in the body is to be present with the Lord." Corinthains 5:8
>
> "It is appointed unto men once to die, but after this the judgment." Hebrews 9:27
>
> "So Christ was sacrificed once to take away the sins of many people, and He will appear a second time, not to bear sin, but to bring salvation to those who are waiting for Him. There is therefore now no condemnation to them which are in Christ Jesus, who walk not after the flesh but after the Spirit." Hebrews 9:28 Romans 8:1

In John 5:24, Jesus said, "Verily, verily, I say unto you, He that heareth My word and believeth on Him that sent Me has everlasting life and shall not come into condemnation, but is passed from death unto life."

CHAPTER 8

The Last Day

*T*he last day. This is a chapter that I was not interested in writing at all. I actually struggled to write it, because to be honest with you, I never cared, worried, or even thought about the last day. As a Christian, I don't plan on being here during the tribulation era. On the last day, or shall I say the end of this world, I will be with the rest of the family. You see, I will be alive with JESUS in HEAVEN forever, and so should you.

All throughout the Bible, when God judged the nations, He got His people out of harm's way. For instance, in Genesis 19:22, the angels told Lot to leave the city of Sodom, because they could not destroy it until Lot left with his family. In fact, if we go back to Genesis 18:23, Abraham, while praying for Sodom, asked the Lord, "Will you destroy the righteous with the wicked?" When I say Abraham was praying, he was actually talking to God face to face. Remember, the Lord and two angels appeared to Abraham to tell him the great news that Sarah would be pregnant. As I said earlier in the book, they had dinner. You should read the whole of Genesis 18.

Anyway, before the Lord left to go back to Heaven, He told Abraham He was going to destroy Sodom and Gomorrah. The reason I am pointing this out is that when we pray, we are actually talking to God. Where God, the Lord Jesus, was with Abraham in the flesh, He is here with us by His Holy Spirit. The Holy Spirit is with you all the time—He sees everything, He knows everything, and He hears your every word. He hears your prayers. And He will speak to you! You can reason with God. It was God who said, "Come now, and let us reason together; though your sins be as scarlet, they shall be as white as snow."

Let's pick it up at Genesis 18:24:

"Perhaps there may be fifty righteous within the city; will you also destroy and not spare the place for the fifty righteous that are therein? That be far from Thee to do after this manner, to slay the righteous with the wicked; that the righteous should be as the wicked. That be far from Thee; shall not the Judge of all the earth do right?" And the Lord said, "If I find fifty righteous within the city, then I will spare the entire place for their sake." (Gen. 18:24–26)

If you continue to read Genesis 18 down to verse 32, Abraham was able to bargain with the Lord to the point that the Lord promised Abraham He would not destroy the city if He found ten righteous within it. But to me the most powerful thing about all of this scripture is that if the Lord had found only ten righteous, He would have spared Sodom. Take a second and think about that—God was going spare the very wicked city of Sodom if He found only ten righteous. That shows that the blessing and safety of the Lord follows the righteous. But sadly, God could not find ten people who were righteous. Now, that doesn't say much for Lot's family. I mean, you do the math—there had to be less than ten godly people in his family alone, because God destroyed Sodom and Gomorrah. And we know his wife was not one of the righteous, because she looked back and was turned into a pillar of salt. Sorry Sister Lot.

Let's move on to another example where God spared the righteous before destruction. If you read Genesis 6–9, we see where God spared Noah and his family before He destroyed every living being on earth the first time. I'm sure you all know the story of Noah's ark. Noah's ark was not just a story—it was a real, live event that actually happened, just like Hurricanes Sandy and Katrina—only a thousand times worse. In fact, the reason we see a rainbow today is to remind us that God will never destroy earth by water again. Every time we see a rainbow, it is a constant reminder of God's promise to us but also a reminder that He got tired of evil. When God had finally had enough of man's evil, He destroyed everything that moved—except the righteous Noah, his family, and every animal in the ark.

Now, that brings us to today—the last day. Again, I will try my best to give you a heads up on end times. As I said, it is not my best subject. Through all my years of Bible study, I focused on things that are above: Jesus, Heaven, and how to get myself and you into Heaven. I will say it again—when the terrible things that you are about to read about happen, I will not be here! Neither should you, if you paid attention and gave yourself to the Lord. The Lord has put it on my heart to discuss this matter as one last-ditch effort to save souls, because some of you still reading to this point have not put your faith and trust in the Lord Jesus Christ. Shockingly enough, you are still holding back your full heart from the One who loves you so very much. Even knowing of the glories of Heaven, and with the love of God now plainly revealed, you are still saying, "It's not for me." Some of you still think to yourself, "I am not ready yet; I will get saved someday." Better yet, some are still thinking, "Save me from what?" And some of us, although we see that times are becoming more and more evil, we still think things will get better.

But here's a simple test: ask yourself, "Have things gotten better since I was a child?" People pushed onto subway tracks for no reason. Shootings after shootings—Columbine; Sandy Hook; Aurora; Munich; Nice (eighty four dead); Orlando (forty-nine dead). Wars and rumors of wars. Meteorite hits (Russia on February 15, 2013). Some of us wonder when Jesus will be coming back.

Because of these questions, the Lord wants me to touch on these end-time events. This way, when these things do happen, you will not be here! If you are here, you will be able to point to this book or, more importantly, get out your Bible and understand what's going on. But my biggest hope is that you will not be here during the evil times to come. The evil of today is just a warning of what is to come. The disciples had the same questions that we do today. The answer you are about read Jesus gave to the disciples. The answer that Jesus gave was the same answer for us today. Some of the things Jesus will speak about have already happened. For instance, the temple they were talking about was destroyed in AD 70. Some of the things Jesus spoke about, like nations rising against nations and love growing cold, are happening today. But the great tribulation that is to come and that will be worse than anything that has ever happened hasn't yet happened. But it will happen, just as Jesus said!

Many will get saved during that time. But that's because they will have understood the Gospel for the first time during that time and will have gotten saved. But we who have trusted the Lord will be long gone before any of the following things happen. God will rapture His church (or in other words, take us to Heaven), and then allow everything you are about to read to take place. Like He did with Noah and Lot's family, the Lord Jesus will get His family off this earth before He destroys it. As you will see, you don't want to be here during the times of evil to come.

One last thing before the Creator Himself answers you: If you heard the Gospel and turned it down, and God raptures the church today, and you are stuck here during the tribulation period, it is too late for you. You will not be able to trust the Lord then. If you say to yourself, "I will get saved during the tribulation," know that you will not. By not trusting God now, you have hardened your heart. During the tribulation, there will be so much confusion that you will put your trust in the false Christ. If you read your Bible, you read this book, you went to church, and so on but you still said no, when we are gone, you will be so confused that you will believe the lie.

Here is 2 Thessalonians 2:8–12:

> And then shall that wicked one be revealed whom the Lord shall consume with the spirit of His mouth and shall destroy with the brightness of His coming. Even him whose coming is after the working of Satan with all power and signs and lying wonders, and with all deceivableness of unrighteousness, and in them that perish because they received not the love of the truth that they might be saved. And for this cause, God shall send them strong delusion that they should believe a lie, that they all might be damned who believed not the truth but had pleasure in unrighteousness.

Stop right there! See that part that says God shall send a strong delusion? I want you to think about that. The antichrist will be able to do all kinds of lying signs—false rising of the dead, calling fire from Heaven, rain from a clear sky.

He will say, "I am Jesus," and many will believe him. And if you're still here, you will believe him too. God will make sure of that, because you didn't want to believe him now while you have a chance.

So, here is one last chance to believe. Here is Matthew 24, or as I call it, the Return of The Real King. Let's start at verse 1 and work our way through the rest of the chapter. I will comment from time to time.

> And as Jesus went out and departed from the temple, His disciples came to Him to show Him the buildings of the temple. And Jesus said unto them, "See ye not all these things? Verily I say unto you, there shall not be left here one stone upon another that shall not be thrown down." And as He sat upon the Mount of Olives, the disciples came unto Him privately, saying, "Tell us, when shall these things be? And what shall be the sign of Your coming and of the end of the world?" And Jesus answered and said unto them, "Take heed that no man deceive you, for many shall come in my name saying 'I am Christ' and shall deceive many. And ye shall hear of wars and rumors of wars; see that ye be not troubled, for all these things must come to pass, but the end is not yet. For nation shall rise up against nation, kingdom against kingdom, and there shall be famines and pestilence and earthquakes in divers places. All these are the beginning of birth pains." (Matt. 24:1–8)

OK, look up at me for a second. I'm sorry, I forgot we are reading a book and I am not preaching a sermon. There is a lot in these few verses. Remember I said that Jesus will talk about things that happened and things that will happen? He told the disciples that the temple would be destroyed and not one stone would be left on top of one another, and that happened in AD 70. Forty years after Jesus said those words, the Romans came into Jerusalem and destroyed the temple.

Next, Jesus talks about things that affect us today. Some of this was happening in His day, but it's more prevalent now. But He wanted to make sure you can clearly see the signs of His coming so that you won't be fooled. OK, let's take a close look at what the Lord said. The first thing is that He warns you about the fake Christ called the antichrist. There is a type of antichrist that runs a cult in Mexico. The name of the cult is Defensores de Cristo, which means Defenders of Christ. The cult is running a sex-slavery ring. The head of the cult had the nerve to say that he was Jesus Christ reincarnated. And he would force young women to give themselves to him. And I don't need to say any more about this evil! This was one of my struggles with writing this chapter. If I were going to talk about the signs of the times, unfortunately I would have to put evil stuff like this into the book. I have to warn you, as Jesus did about the false Christ. This way, when the real Jesus comes, you will know Him.

Now, this guy was not the antichrist—that is to come—but just a tiny sample of how evil the antichrist will be. Then Jesus goes on to say that you will hear of wars and rumors of wars. Also, nations will rise up against nations. Again, that is happening today. Israel is about to bomb Iran because of weapons of mass destruction. Sound familiar? The United States is still in Afghanistan. We just finished fighting with Iraq because of weapons of mass destruction. Egypt is in unrest. Libya is in unrest. The French are bombing Mali even as we speak. Israel just finished bombing targets in Syria. North Korea now has nuclear weapons and is threatening to use them on South Korea and the United States. And only the Lord knows what Russia planning.

You see, all these things are real signs that the end is coming soon. Jesus said, "There shall be famines pestilence and earthquakes in divers places." This has been an interesting week for me. As I've been saying all along, I am not an authority on Bible prophecy. I am more of a Heaven guy and a come-to-Jesus guy. But as I was preparing to write this part of the book, the Lord had me on the Internet, watching the news, reading, looking for different things to show that His words are coming true. Famines, we all know about; we see what's going on in India. Even here in the United States, there are people hungry and homeless. All across America, you can see the long food lines and people living on the street.

Look at what Jesus said about earthquakes in diver's places. I'm just going to name a few. As I said earlier in this book, the earthquake in Japan, which knocked out all those nuclear plants and caused the tsunami, is a sign of the end times. The quake in Haiti—a sign of the end times. We even had an earthquake in New York. Not a big one or anything, but think about it. New York City—an earthquake? Really? January 30, 2013—a magnitude 6.7 earthquake hits northern Chile. February 2, 2013—a magnitude 6.7 earthquake hits Japan. February 9, 2013—a magnitude 6.9 earthquake hits Colombia. Isn't this what Jesus said—"earthquakes in divers places"? Clearly what Jesus said is coming to pass. Also notice the frequency: these last three happened within two weeks of each of each other. Now, some may say that this is a reach. You noticed that all three start with the number six? Chile, 6.7; Japan, 6.7; and Columbia, 6.9? In other words, 666 sounds familiar?

Take a close look at Hurricane Sandy when it hit New York. It was something that had never happened before. They called it the perfect storm. The way it was set up; we'll never forget it. Full moon, high tide, a hurricane uniting with a nor'easter. All these are the beginning of birth pains. As I am writing this book, here is some more stuff. China just cracked down on seventy people—Tibet protests. Israeli forces just broke up the Palestine encampment. February 19, 2013—a 4.9 magnitude earthquake just hit China. I am giving you dates, knowing that by the time this book gets published, things will have gotten much worse. All so that you can read and believe. Remember September 11?

These are the beginning of birth pains. Jesus uses the Greek word *Odin* (pronounced *oh-deen*), which means "pain as in childbearing," translated to "birth pain." This is important, because when a woman's labor pains come and fade, they are called Braxton Hicks pains or false labor. But when the pain gets stronger and stronger, becomes more frequent, and doesn't fade, you are in labor. The baby is coming, and it's time to go to the hospital. Here is the point in the world we live in today: we are past the Braxton Hicks days. These are not false signs; this world is in labor and soon will be destroyed!

OK, let's go back to what Jesus said, starting at Matthew 24:9:

> Then they shall deliver you up to be afflicted and shall kill you, and ye shall be hated of all the nations for my namesake. And then shall many be offended and shall betray one another and

shall hate one another, and many false prophets shall rise and deceive many. And because iniquity shall abound, the love of many shall wax cold. But he that shall endure to the end, the same shall be saved. And this Gospel of the kingdom shall be preached in the entire world for a witness unto all nations, and then shall the end come. When you therefore shall see the abomination of desolation spoken of by the prophet Daniel stand in the holy place (whoever reads it, let him understand), then let them which be in Judea flee into the mountains. Let him which is on the housetop not come down to take anything out of his house. Neither let him which is in the field return back to take his clothes. And woe unto them that are with child and unto them that give suck in those days. But pray that your flight be not in the winter neither on the Sabbath day. For then shall be great tribulation such as was not since the beginning of the world to this time and never ever shall be. And except those days should be shortened, there should no flesh be saved: but for the elect sake, they shall be shortened. Then if any man shall say unto you, "Lo, here is Christ or there," believe it not. For there shall arise false Christs and false prophets and shall and show great signs and wonders insomuch that if it were possible, they shall deceive the very elect. Behold, I have told you before. Wherefore if they shall say unto you, "Behold, he is in the desert," go not forth, or "Behold, he is the secret chambers," believe it not. For as lightning cometh out of the east and shineth even upon the west, so shall also the coming of the Son of Man be. For wheresoever the carcass is, there will be eagles gathered together. (Matt. 24:9–28)

OK, let me put my little two cents in, not that you need to be hearing more from me. Because the King has said it all. Everything you just read, Jesus said over two thousand years ago, but it is happening today, just as Jesus said. Right now, in different Muslim countries, Christians are being delivered up and killed as we speak. In Iran, a pastor named Seed Abedini has been put in jail. His only crime is that he is a Christian. They torture him every day, trying to get him to deny Jesus. There are many false prophets today, just as Jesus said. There are many countries today where if you talk about Jesus, you risk the death penalty. In those countries, when a loved one gets saved, other family members deliver them to the people to be murdered. Some even murder their own family members, calling such murders honor killings.

So, you need to be reminded that to be absent in the body is to be present with the Lord. But as you all know by now, this body will die, but *you* will never die. Jesus also said that because of iniquity, the love of many shall wax cold. You see that today. In other words, people are more cold and unloving today than at any other time. The amazing thing is that God even used popular music to ask the same question. Remember the song "Where Is the Love"? Think about it—you can't even go to the movies and watch a film like *Batman* without some unloving and evil person fueled by the devil shooting up the theater. Or what kind of person calculates how to go to a school full of little children aged six and seven to murder them? Wives are cheating on husbands. Husbands are cheating on their wives. In one instance, a woman from Staten Island in New York left her husband to go on vacation to Turkey. While there, she cheated on her husband with another man she'd met on the Internet. Unfortunately for her, she paid for her sin with her life.

What about the things they're doing to women in other countries? My goodness, you'd better believe that God will judge this. A nine-year-old girl has a baby. A sixty-year-old man marries an eight-year-old child. How about the Argentine young woman who married a man while he was in jail for killing her sister? Her twin sister, no less! Abortion after abortion, even though sonograms clearly show arms, legs, eyes, nose, ears, feet, and heartbeats of little human beings. And you think a pure and Holy God who sees and knows everything is going to let this continue? Really?

I could go on and on, but I think I've made my point. What Jesus is saying is coming true today. Whoever got a nine-year-old girl pregnant? That is not love. A sixty-year-old man marrying an eight-year-old child? That's not love. A man is suspected of killing your twin sister, and you're going to marry him? And this guy was convicted of killing her—he is in jail for it—and you marry him while he is in prison? And you say he's innocent? Really? That's love? Just like Jesus said, "The love of many has waxed cold."

OK—again, take another close look at where Jesus said, "And this Gospel will be preached to all the nations." When Jesus said this over two thousand years ago, the ballpoint pen hadn't even been invented yet. And there definitely wasn't any radio. Yet He said that this Gospel would be preached to all the nations. You see, being God, He knew about cell phones, airplanes, the Internet, billboards, Twitter, and so on, even before they were all invented. Where the disciples might have been perplexed, Jesus knew that we would have these capabilities today. So, what He said two thousand years ago might not have seemed possible or made any sense then, but is very possible today. That's why I laugh when a person takes all this credit for inventing the computer chip, because God gave him this info. And God will use it to get His word out to the entire world before He destroys it. Heaven and earth and Twitter shall pass away, but Jesus's words will remain forever.

Moving right along toward the destruction of the world. As you can see, these are evil times. Kids murdering their parents for their parents' money. Beautiful children leaping to their deaths because they have been bullied. And the amazing thing is that the bullies have no compassion; some even say, "Go ahead, kill yourself." What about today's music? I can remember when they wouldn't show Elvis on TV from the waist down. They were afraid his gyrations were too provocative. Well, today anything goes. We go from beautiful words like "You caught me crying in the chapel" to cuss words that will never be printed by me. I got ninety-nine problems, and I will stop right there.

Oh! And I almost forgot—what about the teachers sleeping with teenagers? Or the famous football coach who molested little boys for years before he was caught? All I can say is that when I was a child, we were able to pray in school. One nation under God. And in those days, there were far fewer murders, much less violence in schools. You never heard of kids shooting each other, and you'd definitely not be sleeping with a teacher. You respected your teacher. And the thought of you having sex with each other was gross to you both. Do you think we should bring prayer back in school? We will not bring prayer back into school. Because of iniquity, the love of many has waxed cold. OK, this brings us to the part where Jesus talks about the abomination of desolation the antichrist.

The antichrist will be the evilest man this world has ever known. He will make Hitler look like a Boy Scout. He will be the devil in a human body. This means that the devil will enter into a man and do all this evil through that man. The arrival of the antichrist will be the start of the tribulation period. But, thank God, we will not be here when his evil is in full bloom. God is going to remove the church, a process which is called the rapture. I am going to give you my quick view on this. There are many books out there on the end times that are better than this one. May the Lord lead you to buy one. They will be better and in more detail. But for the purpose of this book, I will move quickly. Please, again, remember that this is a Heaven book not an end-times book.

Just before the antichrist comes on the scene or shows his true colors, God is going to remove us—all the church—those who put their trust in the Lord Jesus. In an instant, we will be gone into Heaven. The Bible says in the twinkling of an eye. That's not even a full blink. Matthew 24:40: "Then shall two be in the field; the one shall be taken and the other left. Two women shall be grinding at the mill; the one shall be taken and the other left." Think of the chaos! In less than the blink of an eye, billions of people will be gone! Airplanes without pilots, cars without any drivers, trains without motormen. Captains of ships gone! Loved ones gone! And every young child gone! There will be crashes everywhere as never seen before, planes falling from the sky because the pilot was taken. Many planes crashing because the air traffic controllers were Christians, and they are gone. Give it some thought—cars crashing, trains crashing. If a woman is pregnant and she doesn't believe the baby inside her has gone to Heaven, she's left with an empty womb. My wife is a nurse, and she used to work in the nursery. Sometimes they would have twenty babies there at a time. All those kids would be gone! And my wife too. Can you imagine the families screaming for their children? Think of all of the fires that will burn. There will not be enough firefighters the way those guys pray—most of them are saved. I think most if not all would be gone. Cops, teachers, doctors and nurses, mechanics—all gone!

Now, think about this happening all over the entire world, for there are believers in every country. Drink that in, and understand the chaos. Now, look at the economic disaster. If stocks and the Dow Jones take a hit just because Congress can't settle the budget, imagine what will happen when this hits the entire world. I hear all these doomsday people telling you they are prepared. I just read today that a couple was teaching their nine-year-old daughter how to hold an AK-47. They actually show pictures of this cute little girl holding the rifle. This is silly for two reasons. One, the gun was so big the child could barely hold it, much less fire it. Two, chances are that little girl would be taken to Heaven during the rapture. Most nine-year-olds have a pure heart before God. I am telling you now before it happens that you cannot prepare for this. The only preparation is to give your life to Jesus so that you will be gone with the rest of us. Just as Heaven is a real place, these things will surely happen, just as Jesus said. On top of this, food will be scarce, and most of your workforce will be gone. And gas lines—forget about it. I live in New York; the gas lines for Superstorm Sandy were ten to twenty blocks long. It will be like that all over the world, all at once. Think about your worst disasters and multiply the chaos by hundreds. And unless you read this book, your Bible, or an end-times book, you will have no idea what has happened. Imagine looking at the CNN news reports or listening to the radio reports saying that people have just disappeared.

What about Twitter? I remember a Blake Griffin dunk shut Twitter down. Do you think *this* will shut Twitter down? Imagine you're at a Knicks basketball game. Melo, KP, Derrick Rose, Courtney Lee, Noah—the entire team—and every Knicks fan gone! Think about the shock on the Celtic sidelines and to their fans, wondering what just happened. "Where did they go, and why are we still here?" Just kidding—my prayer is that no one would be left behind. In Heaven, there is only one type of fans. Fans of Jesus! What about calling a loved one who was a believer on a cell phone, and then they are gone? What about the mother in the park with her friends and all their children together playing, and instantly they are gone to Heaven? You didn't believe, and now you're left here. Now do you understand the problem this could cause? Can you understand why I've been pleading and sometimes begging that you trust Jesus?

And to the rich and you superstars—your money will not help you. This earth will be jacked up, and I haven't gotten to the antichrist yet. You will trade all your money just to buy something to eat. The entire world economy will have collapsed. Your silver, your gold, your diamonds, your cars, your homes— all will mean nothing. And think of your mind-set when you realize that it's not a dream and that you're still here. Think about the death and destruction resulting from all those people being gone in one shot. There are about 2.1 billion Christians in the world today. That equals about one third of the entire world population. The let's just say for the purposes of this book that every one of them is the real deal, a true believer like myself, along with those of you who have read this book and trusted the Lord. So, that would mean 2.1 billion would be gone in an instant. Do you think that would affect our economy? Our food supply?

I could go on and on about the problems and the devastation this will cause, but I have to move on. Stop here and think about it. The reason I want you to think about it is I want you to make it personal. Think about how this will affect you. Go now and meditate on GOD's word, the Bible. I will wait here. I am a little hungry, so while you are reading, I am going to grab a bite to eat. Read Mathew 24, 1 and 2 Thessalonians, Luke 21, and Mark 13. GOD will give to you even more wisdom from His word than you are getting reading this book. Not many authors will admit this, but I have no problem doing so because it's not about me—it's about GOD and you, His son or daughter. The LORD JESUS is the teacher of us All, and HE is the true author behind this book anyway.

Oh great, you are back. Give me a second. Let me just finish this sandwich. There now, where were we. Oh yes. As I said before, all of us will be gone. That brings us back to the antichrist and the tribulation period. Now, for you Bible scholars and teachers who believe we will be here during tribulation, I understand your concerns, but I do not believe we will be here. You new believers can go have some juice and a slice of pizza if you'd like while I talk to the scholars, pastors, and teachers who think they will be here during tribulation.

When the antichrist arrives or is revealed, we will have seven years of his reign, according to the book of Daniel. The first three and half years will be at peace as the antichrist tries to con the world into believing he is Jesus. Then, after that, for another three and a half years, the antichrist will show his true colors, as we are about to read. Then, right after that, on the seventh year begins the wrath of God. You might get me to believe that Jesus would leave us all here during the phony peace time of the antichrist. It would make sense, because the true believer will know that he is a phony. Thus, since it's a time of peace, He may leave us here to warn the people that this man is a false Christ and not the Messiah.

But sometime before the second three and a half years, we will be gone. In the second three and a half years, the devil will be able to do whatever he wants, and he will murder many. Now, ask yourself this question: Would you leave your child at home with a person you knew was a murderer and who couldn't wait to kill him? On top of that, the killer hated you and tried to kill you but could not. Because he couldn't kill you, you gave up your life so that your child could live. What if the devil knocked on your door and said, "Hi, I am the devil. Do you want me to watch the little one?" Would you say, "Great! Come on in, devil. I made your favorite—devil's food cake"? Of course you wouldn't leave your child with the devil. And God wouldn't either. During that second three and a half years, God will pour out His wrath and judgments. As I said before, God always gets His people out before He pours out His wrath. So, if this will make you happy, you may get seven years with the antichrist. The first three and a half years will be peaceful. Then the next three and a half will be horrible. Sometime before the second three and a half is over or right after, I and the rest of the readers will be long gone, before the evil comes—and you will too! You need to pray and seek out God on this. Here is some scripture that you can read:

> "Because you have kept the word of My patience, I also will keep you from the hour of temptation which shall come upon the entire world, to try them that dwell upon the earth." (Rev. 3:10)
>
> "Watch ye, therefore, and pray always, that ye may be accounted worthy to escape all these things that shall come to pass and stand before the son of man." (Luke 21:36)

Hint: I have too much faith in our Dad Jesus to believe He would leave me with the devil! He promised to never leave me or forsake me.

OK, new believers, you can come back now. I hope you didn't eat too much pizza, because it is about to get really bad. The antichrist, as I said before, will be the devil inside of a man's body. According to the Bible, he will be a man from the Middle East. Again, I am not an end-times guy, but read Daniel 9–12, Ezekiel 38–39; also, the book of Isaiah and Revelation 13 point to a man from the Middle East. He will come in as a man of peace. In fact, he will make world peace. He will be a man of charm. He will have great charisma. And for three and a half years, this entire world will be at peace. Can you imagine Israel, Iran, Iraq, Russia, China, South Korea, North Korea, and the United States all living in peace? No wars; no unrest anywhere. World peace!

He will have everyone fooled. Before he even says it, many people will think that he is the Lord. They will say, "This man has accomplished so much. He has given us world peace." We go from the chaos of the rapture to peace and harmony. The antichrist will have a false prophet. This is a guy who will be telling you how great the antichrist is. The false prophet will be the antichrist's right-hand man. He encourages you to believe this man. For no one has accomplished world peace before him. In fact, the Bible says in Daniel 9 that the antichrist will build the new temple in Jerusalem. Because he has world peace, he will be able to build the new temple on the very same ground, the very same spot, before the Temple Mount. The Arabs and the Jews will be at peace with each other, so they will have no problem with the beast building that temple on the Temple Mount. And I'm sure all the nations will donate money and resources to his glorious temple. And with the machines and stuff we have today, that temple will be glorious indeed. And the false prophet will tell us, "Surely he must be sent from above. This man must be the Messiah."

The antichrist will be full of satanic power and lying wonders. He will build a huge statue in his own image and make it talk. And when I say make it talk, I mean make it come alive and talk, not with electronics and speakers! He will take control of all the money, resources, and food every day. There will be one world currency and then a cashless society. People, we are almost there now—debit cards, credit, and do on. He will be able to make it rain fire from a clear sky. He will rise from the dead. People, this will be no movie; this will be no trick—it will be the devil and his full power. Because the church and the Holy Spirit will be gone, the demons will have their way. So, this earth will fully belong to the devil and his minions. And this phony peace will go on for three and a half years.

And after three and a half years, the lying wonder will show his true colors. Then there will be no more games. The false prophet will be exalting this guy as the Messiah. The antichrist will claim to be God. And he will sit in the new temple and tell the world that he is God the Messiah. He will make a stature in his own image, put in the temple, and force you to worship it. And many will believe he is the Messiah because of the lying wonders and fake resurrection. Anyone who doesn't worship the beast, the antichrist, will be killed. He will force you to take his mark, which is called the mark of the beast in the Bible. You will have to get the mark on your hand or your forehead and by taking his mark, pledge your love, your soul, to the devil, the antichrist.

To keep it simple, the choice will be clear: you will choose the devil, the antichrist; or you will choose the Lord Jesus Christ. Take the mark belonging to the devil. If you don't take the mark, you will be murdered. Without the mark, you will not be able to buy or sell; you will not be able to go anywhere. You must take the mark of the beast to do anything in this country or anywhere in the world. I already see that the world is trying to move toward one world currency—the Euro, for instance. When the antichrist comes on the scene, there will be only his currency—his mark.

Again, I want you to think about something. This is why I love the Word of God. This was spoken by Jesus in the book of Revelation over two thousand years ago. It was written in the book of Daniel before Jesus was born, about 535 BC. As I stated earlier, in those days they didn't have ballpoint pens. Just forty years ago, this scripture couldn't be fulfilled. But now, with today's technology and the use of scanners, do you see where I'm going? GPS, credit cards, microchips—already there are eye retina scanners that you have to look into to get into a building. At the School of Mines and Technology in South Dakota, they are testing a fingerprint-scanning machine. What sets its biocryptology apart is their biometrics. Once the unit scans your finger, it feels for blood pulsing under it. This is to make sure you didn't cut someone's finger off to make the transaction. It feels for a pulse to be sure that the person is living. Now you understand why I say the Bible is true. Jesus warns you of the mark the beast, of scanners, of all this stuff, over two thousand years ago. Jesus knew then that today, the antichrist will be able to track your every move through scanners, GPS, and so on.

> And he exercises all the power of the first beast before him, and causes the earth and them which dwell therein to worship the first beast, whose deadly wound was healed. And he doeth great wonders, so that he makes fire come down from Heaven on the earth in the sight of men, and deceived them that dwell on the earth by the means of those miracles which he had power to do in the sight of the beast; saying to them that dwell on the earth that they should make an image to the beast, which had the wound by the sword and did live. And he had power to give life unto the image of the beast, that the image of the beast should both speak, and cause as many as would not worship the image of the beast to be killed. And he caused all, both small and great, rich and poor, free and bond, to receive a mark in their right hand, or in their foreheads; and that no man might buy or sell, save he that had the mark, or the name of the beast, or the number of his name. Here is wisdom. Let him that hath understanding count the number of the beast: for it is the number of a man; and his number six hundred threescore and six. (Rev. 13:12–18)

Here you have the Bible clearly pointing to a mark, which really will be some type of scanner mark or chip that will be implanted or marked in your forehead or your right hand. The Bible makes the prediction so precise, even to tell you which hand! And the number 666! During this time, the last three and a half years, there will be murder, rape, and ungodly behavior such as this world has never seen. As I said before, what we see today is just the beginning of sorrows and labor pains. Be here in the second three and half years, and the evil will be in full labor. Families will be killing each other to take the mark of the beast.

> But when they shall lead you and deliver you up, take no thought beforehand what ye shall speak, neither do premeditate: but whatsoever shall be given you in that hour, that shall you speak: for it is not you that speak, but the Holy Ghost. Now brother shall betray brother to death, and the father the son; and the children shall rise up against their parents and shall cause them to be put to death. And you shall be hated of all men for My name's sake; but he that shall endure to the end shall be saved. (Mark 13:11–13)

It will be the most wicked times the world has ever seen—three and a half years of killing, murder, rape, and torture all over the world. Christians will be hunted down and killed like dogs in the street, and the world will rejoice with the fake Christ. Many who have read the Bible or a copy of this book will cry out in anguish, "Why didn't I get saved while I had the chance?"

OK, moving right along. Sometime during the apex of this evil time, the Lord Jesus will begin to pour out His judgment on the entire world and then destroy it. I am going to move quickly now as I bring this book to a close. I am going to tell you some of the judgments the rest you can read on your own. There are some seal judgments and some bowl judgments I am going to just touch on some of them but not all, because as I said all along, this is not that type of book. It is a Heaven book, remember, not an end-times book. So, we will close the book the way we have been doing all along. I will give you the Word of the Lord, and then I will expound on what we just read. We will be working quickly through the book of Revelation, starting at chapter 6. These are visions that Lord Jesus gave John about how the world would end. Please remember that Jesus spoke of things that have already happened and of things that will soon happen.

> Now I saw when the Lamb opened one of the seals, and I heard one of the four living creatures saying with a voice like thunder, "Come and see." And I looked and beheld a white horse: he who sat on it had a bow; and a crown was given to him: and he went out, conquering and to conquer. (Rev. 6:1–2)

OK, stop for a second. Some people think the rider on this horse is Jesus. But since this is in the tribulation, I believe this rider represents the antichrist, conquering the world with his lying wonders. Later in this book, Jesus will be riding a white horse, but there will be no doubt it is Jesus the KING OF KINGS and LORD OF LORDS.

> And when he opened the second seal, I heard the second living creature saying, "come and see." Another horse, fiery red, went out. And it was granted to the one who sat on it to take peace from the earth, and that the people should kill one another; and there was given to him a great sword. (Rev. 6:3–4)

OK, stop again. Clearly the Holy Spirit at this point has stopped holding mankind back from sinning, leaving it to its lust for murder, so people are killing each other left and right.

> When he opened the third seal, I heard the third living creature say, "Come and see." So I looked and beheld a black horse; and he who sat on it had a pair of scales in his hand. And I heard a voice in the midst of the four living creatures saying, "A court of wheat for a denarius, and three quarts of barley for a denarius and do not harm the oil and the wine." (Rev. 6:5–6)

OK, obviously this black-horse rider is sent to destroy part of the money. So far we have three seal judgments: we have the antichrist conquering the world; we have peace taken from the world, so people are killing each other; and the world economy is being destroyed!

> When he opened the fourth seal, I heard the voice of the fourth
> living creature saying, "Come and see." So I looked, and be-
> hold, a pale horse. And the name of him who sat on it was
> Death, and Hades followed him. And power was given to them
> over a fourth of the earth to kill with the sword, and with
> hunger, and with death, and by the beasts of the earth. (Rev.
> 6:7–8)

Stop! When you see the word *sword*, think guns, bombs, and swords. So here,
a fourth of the people of the earth are going to die by sword, hunger, and the
animals—animals meaning by lions, tigers, and bears, you die! The devil and
his demons will enter into these animals and use them to kill people. We see
some of that today. I just read an article where a man and a woman were having
sex in the bush of Zimbabwe. A lion attacked them, and the man managed to
run away. The lion killed the woman; the only thing left were mangled remains.
How about the killer whale at SeaWorld that drowned a woman? Or the zoo-
keeper killed by lions? I could go on and on. Today, some of the animals are
under the control of Satan. During the time of the great tribulation, with the
spirit of peace taken away from the earth, the devil will have full control over all
the animals. And he will use them to do his killing. Imagine the chaos—apes,
tigers, cheetahs, whales, sea Lions, sharks, rats, cats, dogs, you name it, all in
the hands of the devil.

Do you see why I had to write this chapter? I couldn't tell you about the
beauty of Heaven without warning you of the hell to come. For some of my
older readers, remember Alfred Hitchcock's film *The Birds*? How about *Willard*?
This will be a thousand times worse. And this will be the real deal, not just a
movie! Anyway, we are still in Revelation 6:

> And when he had opened the fifth seal, I saw under the altar
> the souls of those who have been slain for the word of God and
> for the testimony which they held. And they cried with a loud
> voice, saying, "How long, O Lord, holy and true, until you
> judge and avenge our blood on those who dwell on the earth?"

> Then a white robe was given to each of them; and it was said to
> them that they should rest a little while longer, until both the
> number of their fellow servants and their brethren, who would
> be killed as they were, was completed. (Rev. 6:9–11)

Stop! This is great scripture. Here we see the people in Heaven given a white robe. And they know what's going on on earth. In fact, they ask the Lord, "When will You take vengeance for us?" As you can see, they have bodies; if they were just spirits, why would they need a robe? These were martyred saints that had died and gone to Heaven up into the time when John wrote the book of Revelation and some of the martyred saints out of tribulation. Jesus showed John saints of the past and of the future. And as you can see, although they are told to rest here for a while, they are very much alive and not sleeping in the grave.

> I looked when he opened the sixth seal (Rev. 6:12).

OK, we can stop right here. These last beautiful verses of Revelation 6 are the main theme of this chapter: "the last day." They are verses 12–16. But I cannot give them to you yet, because I have to fill in some more blanks. We will get back to them, I promise.

Moving right along, Revelation 7 opens up with the living God putting His seal upon the 144,000 Jewish virgin men. Of the tribe of Judah, 12,000 were sealed; of the tribe of Reuben, 12,000 were sealed; 12,000 was sealed of the tribe of Gad; 12,000 were sealed of the tribe of Asher; 12,000 more were sealed of the tribe of Naphtali; 12,000 were sealed of the trial of the Manasseh; 12,000 were sealed of the tribe of Simeon; 12,000 were sealed of the tribe of Levi; 12,000 of tribe of Issachar; 12,000 were sealed of the tribe Zebulon; 12,000 of the tribe Joseph; and last but not least, 12,000 of the tribe of Benjamin. I believe the Lord is going to use this 144,000 to reach the lost of Israel during the time of tribulation. Not only Israel, but anyone who will believe. All right, let's continue to move forward toward destruction:

After these things I looked, and behold, a great multitude which no one could number, of all nations, tribes, peoples, and tongues, standing before the throne and before the Lamb, clothed with white robes, with palm branches in their hands, and crying out with a loud voice saying, "Salvation belongs to our God who sits on the throne, and to the Lamb!" All the angels stood around the throne, and the elders and the four living creatures, and fell on their faces before the throne and worshipped God, saying, "Amen! Blessing and glory and wisdom, thanksgiving and honor and power and might be to our God forever and ever. Amen." Then one of the elders answered, saying to me, "Who are these which are arrayed in white robes, and where did they come from?" And I said to him, "Sir, you know." So he said to me, "These are the ones that shall come out of the great tribulation, and wash their robes and make them white in the blood of the Lamb." (Rev. 7:9–14)

Stop. So you see, many people will be saved during the tribulation period. But I would rather get saved now! Because some of these saints, after getting saved during tribulation, will have, I am sad to say, their heads cut off. OK, we are still filling in the blanks, moving quickly and heading toward the end and the last day. Revelation 8 talks about the trumpet and censer judgments.

The first angel sounded his trumpet, and there came hail, and fire followed, mangled with blood, and they were thrown down to the earth; and a third of the trees were burned up, and all the green grass was burned. (Rev. 8:7)

Stop. There go all those beautiful golf courses! Burned up and covered with blood!

And the second angel sounded his trumpet, and something like a great mountain burning with fire was thrown into the sea, and a third of the sea became blood. And a third of the living creatures in the sea died. And a third of the ships were destroyed. (Rev 8:8–9)

Stop. A meteorite will hit the earth. This meteorite will destroy a third of the world's fish population and a third of the world's navy.

And the third angel sounded his trumpet, and a great star fell from Heaven, burning like a torch, and it fell on a third of the rivers and on the springs of water. The name of this star is Wormwood. A third of the waters become Wormwood. And many men died from the water because it was made bitter. Then the fourth angel sounded his trumpet, and a third of the sun was struck, a third of the moon, and a third of the stars, so that a third of them were darkened, and a third of the day did not shine and likewise the night. (Rev 8:10–12)

Stop! Again, I want you to think about what you just read. A third of the sun, a third of the moon, a third of the stars not shining; simply put, a third of the earth dark and freezing cold. If I had to guess, thirty degrees below zero and total darkness!

And I looked, and I heard an angel flying from the midst of Heaven, saying with a loud voice, "Woe! Woe! Woe to the inhabitants of the earth, because of the remaining blasts of the trumpet and of the three angels that are about to sound." (Rev 8:13)

Stop! Look at God's mercy. In the middle of this mess, He uses one of His angels to warn those who are alive of their coming woe! It's almost like the angel feels sorry for us. It's almost like his mind is blown by what is about to come next. Well, here it is:

Then I saw the fifth angel sound his trumpet, and I saw a star fall from Heaven to earth and was given the key to the bottomless pit. When he opened the bottomless pit, smoke rose out of the pit like the smoke of a great furnace. So the sun and the air were darkening because of the smoke of the pit. Then out of the smoke, locusts came upon the earth. And to them was given power, as the scorpions of the earth have power. (Rev 9:1–3)

Stop! These were demonic insects, crossbred between a locust and a scorpion. They could fly and cause you the tremendous pain of a scorpion sting.

They were commanded not to harm the grass of the earth, or any green thing, or any tree, but only those who do not have the seal of God on their foreheads. (Rev. 9:4)

Stop! But as you can see, God is still in control, because they were told they could not harm God's people or any green thing. Let's continue on this fast-moving train as the last day motors on. The next seven verses are mind-boggling.

And they were not given authority to kill them but to torment them for five months. Their torment was like the torment of a scorpion when it strikes a man. In those days, men will seek death and will not find it. They will desire to die, and death will flee from them. (Rev. 9:5–6)

Stop! Stop! Stop! Did you get that? When this being stings people, they will be in so much pain that they will want to die, but God will not allow them to die. Death will flee from them. In those days, men and women with the mark of the beast will try to commit suicide, but God won't let them die for at least five months. People will shoot themselves in the head, jump in front of trains, cars, and so on, overdosing on drugs—whatever—trying to escape life, only to find out that they can't die and have made things worst. Now your body is more broken, in more pain from the fall, gunshot, or whatever, but you cannot die! Imagine—you blow half your head off, but you are still alive, looking like a mess and feeling every pain! Wow!

> They had tails like scorpions, and there were stings in their tails. Their power was to hurt men for five months. And they had as king over them the angel of the bottomless pit, whose name in Hebrew is Abaddon, but in Greek he has the name Apollyon. (Rev. 9:10–11)

Stop! I could go on and on with the death and destruction, but here is the bottom line: some people will never repent. While all of this going on, God in His grace and mercy is still trying to save. For instance, in the next woe, the Lord sends four angels and two hundred million horsemen to kill another third of mankind. But look what the Bible says in Revelation 9:20–21:

> But the rest of mankind, who were not killed by these plagues still did not repent of the works of their hands; they did not stop worshipping demons, and idols of gold and silver, brass, stone, and wood, which can neither see nor hear nor walk. And they did not repent of their murders or their sorceries or their sexual immorality, or their thefts.

Stop and think about it. The Lord could just destroy the earth in one shot. But in His mercy, He is still trying to reach the lost. After all of this, Jesus will send two witnesses from Heaven. How many of your friends and loved ones say to you that they believe the Lord sends someone from Heaven? The truth is that if they are here during this time, they still wouldn't believe. In fact, they would probably try to kill God's messenger from Heaven. Look at Revelation 11:3:

> "And I will give power to two witnesses, and they will prophesy 1,260 days, clothed in sackcloth." These are the two olive trees and the two lampstands standing before the God of the

earth. And if anyone wants to harm them, fire proceeds from their mouths and devours their enemies. And if anyone wants to harm in this manner, he must be killed. These have the power to shut Heaven so that no rain will fall in the days of their prophesy; and they have power over the waters to turn them to blood, and to strike the earth with all plagues as often as they desire. When they have finished their testimony, the beast that ascends out of the bottomless pit will make war against them, overcome them, and killed them. And their dead bodies will lie in the street of the great city, which is spiritually called Sodom and Egypt, where also our Lord was crucified. And they of the people, kindred, tongues, and nations will see their dead bodies for three and a half days, and will not allow the dead bodies to be put in graves. And those who dwell on the earth will rejoice over them and make merry, and send gifts one to another, because these two prophets tormented those who dwell on the earth. Now after three and a half days, the breath of life from God entered them, and they stood on their feet, and a great fear fell on those who saw them. And then they heard a loud voice from Heaven saying to them, "Come up here," and they ascended to Heaven in a cloud, and their enemies saw them. In that same hour, there was a great earthquake, and a tenth of the city fell. In the earthquake, seven thousand people were killed, and the rest were afraid and gave glory to God. (Rev. 11:3–13)

Stop! Here you have the devil's Christmas. The two witnesses die, and the world rejoices and gives gifts to each other. Then the two men of God come back alive and go back to Heaven. But before they go, they leave the world a gift: a huge earthquake that destroys a tenth of Jerusalem and seven thousand thousand people. But God, who is rich and merciful, not wanting anyone to perish, will again reach for the undecided vote! But if you have taken the mark, your goose is cooked—and I mean cooked. As you will soon see, literately cooked!

God will send three angels to proclaim the Gospel one last time. It will be the one last time to get saved.

> Then I saw another angel flying in the midst of Heaven, having the everlasting Gospel to preach unto them that dwell on the earth; and to every nation, and tongue, and people, saying with a loud voice, "Fear God and give Glory to Him, for the hour of His judgment has come; and worship Him who made Heaven and earth, the sea, and springs of water." Then another angel followed, saying, "Babylon is fallen, is fallen, that great city, because she has made all the nations drink of the wine of the wrath of her fornication." Then a third angel followed them, saying with a loud voice, "If anyone worships the beast and his image, and receive his mark on his forehead or on his hand, he himself shall also drink of the wine of the wrath of God, which is poured out full strength into the cup of his indignation. And he shall be tormented with fire and brimstone in the presence of the holy angels and in the presence of the Lamb. And the smoke of their torment ascends forever and ever; and they have no rest day or night, who worship the beast and his image, and whoever receives the mark of his name." (Rev. 14:6–11)

OK, look up at me for second. Sorry, I did it again—this is a book. One day maybe the Lord will allow me to speak at your church, and we will all laugh about this. Anyway, how many of you would have repented by now? Better question is, how many of you *have* repented by now? Can you believe that the people of this world will still want to fight against God? So God will pour out what is called the bowl judgments, and I don't mean Honey Nut Cheerios!

> Then I heard a loud voice from the temple saying to the seven angels, "Pour out the seven bowls of the wrath of God on the earth." So the first went and poured out his bowl on the earth, and a foul and loathsome sore came upon the men who had the

mark of the beast, those who worshipped is his image. Then
the second angel poured out his bowl on the sea, and it became
as the blood of a dead man, and every living creature in the sea
died. (Rev. 16:1–3)

Stop! You'll notice that this verse says all of the living creatures in the sea died.
Before it was a third; now it is all. Also notice that everybody who took the
mark is covered with sores! That's because at this point, God is done trying to
reach anyone and is in full wrath-of-God mode.

Then the third poured out his bowl on the rivers and springs
of water, and they became as blood. And I heard the angel on
the waters saying: "You are righteous, O Lord, the One who is
and who was and who is to be, because You have judged these
things. For they have shed the blood of saints and prophets, and
You have given them blood to drink, for it is their just due."
And I heard another from the altar saying, "Even so, Lord God
Almighty. True and righteous are Your judgments." Then the
fourth angel poured out his bowl on the sun, and power was
given to him to scorch men with fire. And men were scorched
with great heat, and they blasphemed the name of God who has
the power over these plagues; and they did not repent and give
Him glory. Then the fifth angel poured his bowl on the throne
of the beast, and his kingdom became full of darkness; and they
gnawed their tongues because of the pain. They blasphemed
the God of Heaven because of their pains and their sores and
did not repent of their deeds. (Rev. 16:4–11)

Stop! As you can see, at this point those who have taken the mark are truly the
devil's sons and daughters. They have no place with or use for God or His people. So, all the leaders of this world and all the kingdoms of this world will unite
and stage one last fight against God and His people. The battle of Armageddon.
This is at the Mount of Megiddo at the upper entrance to the Plain of Esdraelon,

Israel's chief battlefield in ancient times. I am eyewitness that this battlefield is still there today. I made a DVD of my wife and I walking through this field in May 2010. OK, read on.

> Then the sixth angel poured out his bowl on the great river Euphrates, and the water was dried up so that the way of the kings of the East might be prepared. And I saw three unclean spirits' platforms coming out of the mouth of the dragon, out of the mouth of the beast, and out of the mouth of the false prophet. They are the spirits of demons performing signs, which go out to the kings of the earth and of the whole world, to gather them to the battle of that great day of God almighty. "Behold, I am coming as a thief. Blessed is he who watches, and keeps his garments, lest he walk naked and they see his shame." And they gathered them together to the place called in Hebrew Armageddon. (Rev. 16:12–16)

Stop. I want you to meditate on what you just read. Now, imagine all the nations in the whole world—Russia, China, India, Japan, the United States, Jordan, Syria, Iran, Iraq, Israel, Great Britain, France—all of them. Now imagine all their tanks, missiles, ships, and nuclear bombs in this valley, ready to fight against God. Think of all the nations of the world with their missiles pointed at this valley, open to destroying the Lord Jesus Christ. Planes, drones, you name it, all waiting for the command of the antichrist. And quicker than the heavy-weight champion's ten-second knockout in the first round, here is what happens next. Turn in your Bible to Revelation 19, starting at verse 11:

> Now I saw Heaven opened, and behold, a white horse. And He who sat on it is called Faithful and True, and in righteousness He judges and makes war. His eyes are like a flame of fire, and on His head are many crowns. And He has a name written that no man knows but He Himself. And He is clothed with a vesture dipped in blood: and His name is called the word

of God. And the armies which were in Heaven followed Him upon white horses and clothed and fine linen, white and clean. (Rev. 19:11–14)

OK, stop again for a second. Here we have the Lord Jesus Christ coming back with all the Christians who are in Heaven today. We will be riding white horses, and we will be clothed in white. Here is a hint for you to know that this won't be a fight. We are all clothed in white, and I doubt that the Lord wants to get us dirty. And He makes this clear by stating in the scripture that we will be clothed in fine linen—keywords: clean and white. Because having gone to the cross and having shed His blood, He has given mankind every chance to repent. He is God. Can I preach this part? The Bible says that He took away the sins of the world. He is done getting dirty for us! Oh, somebody needs to hear this again. The Bible says that He took away the sins of the world. He is done getting dirty for us! And God's people said Amen! Anyway, add to that all the innocent blood that mankind has shed, from Abel to that Day of Judgment. He is done fooling around. OK, read on.

And out of His mouth goeth a sharp sword, that with it He should smite the nations, and He shall rule them with a rod of iron: and He treadeth the wine press of the fierceness and the wrath of Almighty God. And He had on His vesture and on His thigh a name written: KING OF KINGS and LORDS OF LORDS. (Rev. 19:15–16)

Stop! This is Jesus! The King of Kings and Lord of Lords! OK, continue.

And I saw an angel standing in the sun; and he cried with a loud voice, saying to all the fowls that fly in the midst of Heaven, "Come and gather yourselves together unto the supper of the Great God. that ye may eat the flesh of kings and the flesh of captains, and the flesh of mighty men, and the flesh of horses, and of them that sit on them, and the flesh of all men, both free and bond, both small and great." And I saw the beast and the kings of the earth and their armies gathered together to make war against him that sat on the horse and against his army. And the beast was taken, and with him the false prophet that wrought miracles before him, with which he deceived them that received the mark of the beast, and them that worshipped his image. These both were cast alive into a lake of fire burning with fire and brimstone. And the remnants were slain with the sword of Him that sat upon the horse, which the sword proceeded out of His mouth; and all the fowls were filled with their flesh. (Rev. 19:17–21)

And now, with that groundwork laid, we can go back to pick up Revelation 16:17: Also you can now read verses Rev. 6:12 -17. Special thanks to editor Sylvia because I almost forgot to get back to Revelation 6:12-17 lol but she reminded me, with her ground work laid sentence. Thanks Sylvia! Revelation 6:12 - 17 and Revelation 16:17 - 21 are the end of the Battle of Armageddon. But as you can see a lot of things happened before we get to the end. That's why I had to fill in the blanks sort to speak. Revelatoin 6:12-17 is the start of the first round and Revelation 16:17-21 is the end of the round. Here it is the First Round Knock out! The end of the Battle of Armageddon! Rev 6:12-17 And I beheld when he had opened the sixth seal, and, lo, there was a great earthquake; and the sun became black as sackcloth of hair, and the moon became as blood;

And the stars of heaven fell unto the earth, even as a fig tree casteth her untimely figs, when she is shaken of a mighty wind.

And the heaven departed as a scroll when it is rolled together; and every mountain and island were moved out of their places.

And the kings of the earth, and the great men, and the rich men, and the chief captains, and the mighty men, and every bondman, and every free man, hid themselves in the dens and in the rocks of the mountains;

And said to the mountains and rocks, Fall on us, and hide us from the face of him that sitteth on the throne, and from the wrath of the Lamb:

For the great day of his wrath is come; and who shall be able to stand?

Revelation 16:17-21 And the seventh angel poured out his vial into the air, and there came a great voice out of the temple of Heaven from the throne saying, "It is done." Then there were voices, and thunders, and lightnings; and there was a great earthquake, such as was not since men were upon the earth, so almighty an earthquake, and so great. And the great city was divided into three parts, and the cities of the nations fell; and great Babylon came in remembrance before God, to give unto her the cup of the wine of the fierceness of His wrath. And every island fled away, and the mountains were not found. And then fell upon man a great hail out of Heaven, and every stone about the weight of a talent, and they blasphemed God because of the lake of the hail, for the plague thereof was exceedingly great.

OK. So, as you can see, that was not much of a fight. I pointed out earlier that the sword in His mouth represents God's word. Here's the bottom line: when Jesus says, "It is done,"   the stars will fall from the sky down to earth. There will be the greatest earthquake ever! The heavens, sun, moon, planets, will roll up and fall down like a cheap shade. The beast and the false prophet will be cast into the lake of fire, and the earth and all those that took the mark will be dead. The earth will be one big garbage dump, without form and void. And what is left will be covered with dead bodies. Then vultures, eagles, and whatever bird that likes to eat flesh will feast on the dead bodies.

I beheld the earth, and lo, it was without form, and void; and the Heavens, and they had no light. I beheld the mountains, and lo, they trembled, and all the hills moved lightly. I beheld, and lo, there was no man, and the birds of the Heaven were fled. I beheld, and lo, the fruitful place was a wilderness, and all the cities thereof where broken down at the presence of the Lord, and by His fierce anger. For thus hath the Lord said, "The whole land shall be desolate; yet will I not make a full end. For this shall the earth mourn, and the Heavens are black; because I have spoken it, I have purposed it, and will not repent; neither will I turn back from it." (Jer. 4:23–28)

But Ed, what about the devil? I am glad you asked. Here is the scripture: Revelation 20.

And I saw angel come down from Heaven, having the key to the bottomless pit and a great chain in his hand. And he laid hold on the dragon, that old serpent, which is the devil, or Satan, and bound him for a thousand years, and cast him into the bottomless pit, and shut him up, and set a seal upon him, that he should deceive the nations no more, until the thousand years should be fulfilled; and after that he is loosed a little season. And I saw thrones, and they that sat on them, and judgment was given unto them; and I saw the souls of them that were beheaded for the witness of Jesus, and for the word of God, and which had not worshipped the beast, neither his image, neither received his mark upon their foreheads, or in their hands; and they lived with Christ a thousand years. But the rest of the dead lived not again until the thousands years were finished. This is the first resurrection. Blessed and holy is he that hath part in the first resurrection; on such the second death hath no power, but they shall be priests of God and of Christ, and shall reign with Him a thousand years. And when a thousand years are expired, Satan shall be loosed out of his prison, and shall go out to deceive the nations which are in the four quarters of the earth, Gog and Magog, to gather them together to battle; the number of whom is as the sand of the sea. And they went up on the breath of the earth and compassed the camp of the saints about, and the beloved city, and fire and brimstone devoured them. And the devil that deceived them was cast into the lake of fire and brimstone, where the beast and the false prophet are, and shall be tormented day and night, forever and ever. And I saw a great white throne, and Him who sat on it, from whose face the earth and the Heaven fled away; and there was found no place for them. And I saw the dead, small and great, stand before God; and the books were opened: and another book was opened, which is the book of life: and the dead were judged out of those things which were written in the books, according to their works. And the sea gave up the dead who were in it; and death and hell delivered up the dead who were in them: and they were judged, every man according to their works, and death and hell were cast into the lake of fire. This is the second death. And whosoever was not found written in the book of life was cast into the lake of fire. (Rev. 20:1–15)

OK, just to go over what we just read in Revelation 20, the earth is totally destroyed. An angel comes from Heaven, chains the devil up, and throws him into the bottomless pit. He shuts the devil up. And to make sure the devil cannot talk, He puts a seal on him. The devil is kept in this prison for a thousand years. Then John is shown all the Christians from the beginning of time to the end of time, reigning with Jesus in Heaven for a thousand years. We know this because, number one, he talked about people who didn't take the mark or worship the image of the beast, who are the people who will be saved during the tribulation that is to come, or shall I say, end-of-the-world saints. Number two, he said blessed and holy is he that hath part in the first resurrection; on such the second death hath no power, but they shall be priests of God and of Christ, and shall reign with Him a thousand years. Clearly here he is talking about God's people who are in Heaven, a real place.

So, here we have God's people with Him in Heaven for a thousand years in the New Jerusalem. Some think that the millennium reign will be here on earth, but at this point, the earth is destroyed, without form, and void. The land is totally desolate, with a giant bottomless pit and the devil chained to it. Remember, there are no moon, no stars, no sun—just black, according to Jeremiah 4:23–28. So, we are in Heaven with Jesus for a thousand years, and then the devil will be loosed for one last time. Then, because he is so dumb, he will deceive the people in hell one last time. Remember, the earth is destroyed with no living beings, because after a thousand years, even those birds that ate the dead flesh will have died off. Earth at that point is really just a holding cell for hell—the condemned dead and the devil. So, when the devil is loosed, the only people he will fool are those he was able to fool before: his people in hell. Because that's all he will have left—the earth will be dead and not able to sustain life. The people in Heaven are God's holy people. I hope you don't mind my quoting The Who: "And we won't be fooled again!"

> And when a thousand years are expired, Satan shall be loosed out of his prison, and shall go out to deceive the nations which are in the four quarters of the earth Gog and Magog, to gather them together to battle; the number of whom is as the sand of the sea. (Rev. 20:7–8)

Stop for a second. You notice it said the nations that are in the earth. That's because they are in hell in the earth. There are no live human beings on the old ravaged earth, and the new one is not built yet. Also, all the birds have died off after a thousand years of no food. After a thousand years, there was nothing living on the earth.

> And they went up on the breath of the earth and compassed the camp of the saints about, and the beloved city, and fire came down from God out of Heaven, and devoured them. And the devil that deceived them was cast into the lake of fire and brimstone, where the beast and the false prophet are, and shall be tormented day and night, forever and ever. (Rev. 20:9–10)

So, here is what happened. The devil is loosed for a season; he convinces the people in hell to try one more time to kill God and His people. When the Lord brings them out the graves from hell for the final white throne judgment—there will be people everywhere, covering the earth and some in Heaven, right

114

outside the New Jerusalem, waiting to be judged. Just before the white throne judgment, these knuckleheads will try their X man last stand (X in this case means marked for second death}. My guess is that just before the books are opened, the devil will say something like, "Look, we are back, just as I said! I resurrected you as I said! I am the beast who was and is now! We got them surrounded—let's get them!"

Now, here is the end of this chapter. The White Throne Judgment! Or you can call it The Lake of Fire Day! Or you call it The Last Day! And first ones to get theirs? The unholy trinity of the beast, the false prophet, and the devil!

> And the devil that deceived them was cast into the lake of fire and brimstone where the beast and the false prophet are, and shall be tormented day and night, forever and ever. (Rev. 20:10)

Then the old earth and the old heavens disappear into thin air, and the rest of these jokers get theirs:

> And I saw a great white throne, and Him that sat on it, from whose face the earth and Heaven fled away; and there was found no place for them. And I saw the dead, small and great, stand before God; and the books were opened, and another book was opened, which is the book of life; and the dead were judged out of those things which were written in the books, according to their works. And the sea gave up the dead which were in it; and death and hell delivered up the dead which were in them; and they were judged every man according to his works. And death and hell were cast into the lake of fire. This is the second death. And whosoever was not found written in the book of life was cast into the lake of fire. (Rev. 20:11–15)

> And I saw a New Heaven and a New Earth, for the first heaven and the first earth had passed away; and there was no more sea. And I, John, saw the holy city, the New Jerusalem, coming

down from GOD out of Heaven, prepared as a bride adorned for husband. And I heard a great voice in Heaven saying, "Behold the tabernacle of God is with men, and He will dwell with them, and they shall be His people. God Himself shall be with them and be their God. And God shall wipe away all of their tears from their eyes; and there shall be no more death, neither sorrow, nor crying, neither shall there be any more pain; for the former things are passed away." And He that sat upon the throne said, "Behold, I make all things new. And He said unto me, "Write this down, for these words are true and faithful." (Rev. 21:1–5

Final Words

I pray that your heart is encouraged! I hope that I was able to answer some of your questions. Let me challenge you to read this book again. Like the bible, you will be surprise at how much more you see and understand, after reading it again. That's because this book is so rich in God's Word. I pray that some of your grief is lifted and your heart is filled with hope. Hope to have confidence to go forward. Go forward knowing your future with God so much brighter than you can imagine. I know for me when I understood how real God and our future home Heaven is, I was able to go on with my life. When my childhood sweet heart Laverne went to Heaven I had no hope I thought that she was lost forever. I was 13 and she was 14 when we started dating. I can say it now because she can't get me but yes she was robbing the cradle. We got married when I was twenty and just after she turned thirty two she was gone! I was an angry widow alone with a eight year old son at 31. But after God revealed His unfailing Love, and the reality of Heaven to me; I realized that she has it way better than you and I. I was able to get married again to my wonderful wife Neyra. Through her I gained another son and twin daughters. My sons got married and I gained two more daughters. One of my daughters got married and I gained a son. My oldest son and his wife had a son now I have a grandson. I pray the same for you. I hope that some of the void is filled knowing that your loved one is alive more than ever! I hope that you have a better understanding about God and our home Heaven. I pray that deep in your heart you will be free to love and live again. I hope that now when someone says to you that they are in a better place you now know they really are in a better place! Those words use to be so shallow, so hollow, to me. Now are so real so true! To everyone that reads, or worked on this book, from my dear sister Josie to every one at

Creative Space. Timothy, Magen, Sylvia,Kimberly to name a few; this was a divine appointment. Before any of us was born, before the foundations of the world God knew that this book would be written. He knows who will be the first one to buy this book. And he knows who will be the last one to read it, before he returns to come get us all! He had me write it because He LOVES YOU! And finally to take all of the sting of of death. Because the truth is you will never die! And some day we will be with Jesus forever! I truly love you all but God loves you so much more! "Write this down for these words are true and Faithful." (Rev. 21-5

My Oscar Emmy Moment

I call this my Oscar Emmy moment because this where I get to say thank you and I want to thank so many people. I want to thank you the reader first. Thank you from the bottom of my heart for buying and reading this book. Without you none of this would be possible. You are the main reason why I wrote this book. So that you would know the truth, and the truth would set you free. Thank You! For those of you that gave your life to the Lord Jesus,Thank you! Your life will never be the same and you haven't seen nothing yet. To my wife Neyra, my sons Eddie, Josh, Andrew, grandson James, and daughters Neyra Jr., Naomi, Stacyann, Ivelise, thank you for your love and support. To my co- author spiritual twin sister Josie thank you. To my three moms Hazel who is in Heaven with God, Pearl (and she really is a pearl of a mom) and Anna, Thank you so much! For what you might ask for just being moms! Moms are special and this is my Oscar Moment. I like to thank my two dads Victor my wife Neyra's dad who is in Heaven and My dad Marshall who I hope to see in Heaven Thank you Men I learned how to be a man from you both. Dads are special, and you got it,this my Emmy moment. I want to thank my brothers Nat, Vincent, and Carl. Vincent is in Heaven with my brother Anthony whom I never met. These guys kept me safe and were all father figures when I was growing up. My nephew little Nat I can not wait to see you some day. You lived here in the hospital for three days then went to the Lord but I never forgot you. Thanks to my sister Isabel the real rock of the family. Her wonderful husband Carl who helped me to keep it together just long enough for God to grab a hold of me. Oh no! The readers are playing the get off the stage music! Thank you Bill, Aggie, Stephen, Thank! you!To my many aunts uncles nieces nephews William, Christine, I love you all My cousins Kim, Vicky, Donald, Dee girl,

George Jr, Janice, Todd, Aunt Alter, all my Tampa Florida Family, Bam, Tiba, Banetta, Wilber, I love you! Aunt Isabel in Heaven, Aunt Gloria in Heaven, Aunt Mary Jane in Heaven see you soon! Hi Sisters Amber, Arica, JoAnn, My brothers Dexter, Derek godson Ethan, goddaughter Ariel, Aunt Margaret uncle Robert, Sister Barbara, Little Vincent, Ranesha, Malisa, Ianna, Zakia. Hi Cheryl, Errol, Jennifer, Carol, Patrick, Christopher, Apples, Daniel, Keith, Darrel, thank you family!Fair Weather Richard and Natalie Thank you! Thank you Amazon.com and every one at Creative space. They are very Creative and to Sylvia brilliant editor who took time out of her busy schedule and made space for me. She encouraged me to write some closing words but now she probably wish she didn't. Lol! Thank You! To all of the pastors and leaders of faith thank you, keep fighting the good fight of faith!Brother Whiteside, Sister Whiteside, Pastor Frank, Pastor Marcus, Pastor Juan, Pastor Hantz, Pastor Subash, Pastor West, Pastor Donnie, Pastor Louis, Pastor Woodside, Pastor Howard thank you all for sowing into my life. God richly bless you and your families. Doug and Hillary thank you! You Doug for always asking about the book which kept me encouraged. Hillary when your mom went to Heaven,you showed me that this book could help someone by your kind words after reading the raw copy. Those on my block Ralph, Wille, Diane, Mary, Jospeh to name a few this book is for you! Shout to PS 124, Jr High School 51 and Automotive High School! To my Con Ed family I see you guys every day and you know how I feel. Howard, Trish, Jimmy, Jamel, Tony, Mike, Neil, Marion, Issa, Dawayne, Stella, Crystal, John, Andre, Eddie, Frank, Cliff, Mel, Dave, Albert, Tommy Hart, Dennis, Chris, Scott, Charles, Nelson, Bruce, Jack, Larkins, Joe D., Sammy, Otis, Karen, Mr President, Fransicos, John, Richee, Bobby, Paul, Gregg, Dean, Igor, Danny, Shirley, Joe thanks for being there everyday! If I missed anyone I am sorry. But before I go let please say this. To all the families who have lost loved ones on September 11, 2001. WE WILL NEVER EVER FORGET!!!! I love you! God Bless You! And God Bless The United States of America!

38679212R00079

Made in the USA
Middletown, DE
23 December 2016